Past Poets
– Future Voices

2010 Poetry Competition for 11-18 year-olds

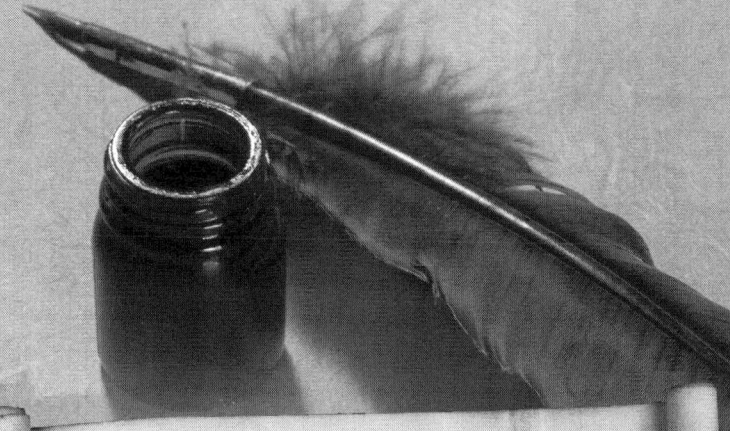

Southern & Eastern England

Edited by Allison Jones

First published in Great Britain in 2010 by

Young**Writers**
Remus House
Coltsfoot Drive
Peterborough
PE2 9JX
Telephone: 01733 890066
Website: www.youngwriters.co.uk

All Rights Reserved
Book Design by Ali Smith & Tim Christian
© Copyright Contributors 2010
SB ISBN 978-0-85739-186-5

Foreword

Young Writers was established in order to promote creativity and a love of reading and writing in children and young adults. We believe that by offering them a chance to see their own work in print, their confidence will grow and they will be encouraged to become the poets of tomorrow.

Our latest competition 'Past Poets - Future Voices' was specifically designed as a showcase for secondary school pupils, giving them a platform with which to express their ideas, aspirations and passions. In order to expand their skills, entrants were encouraged to use different forms, styles and techniques.

Selecting the poems for publication was a difficult yet rewarding task and we are proud to present the resulting anthology. We hope you agree that this collection is an excellent insight into the voices of the future.

Contents

Kenny Izatt (13) 1
Rebecca Thomas 2

Aldworth Science College, Basingstoke
Matt Grimston (12) 4
Jamie Young (11) 5
Rhiannon Michelle Taylor (12) 6
Lucy Peters (11) 7
Elliott Kerwick (12) 8
Oliver Sayer (12) 9
Daniel Reid (12) 10
Elsa Anderson 11
Lauren Wiltshire (12) 12
Harlie-Jaine Rolfe (12) 13
Ben Cossar (11) 14
Bradley Lambell (12) 15
Heidi Padoin (12) 16
George Jones 17
Daniel Goodenough (12) 18
Ryan Parker (12) 19
Musa Ahmad (11) 20
Ollie Shaw (12) 21
Isabelle Kersley (12) 22
Courtney Edenbrow (12) 23
Amber Burton (12) 24
Rabin Magar (12) 25
Robert Scott (11) 26
Brian Radwell (12) 27
Thomas Gammell (12) 28
Bethany Stevens (12) 29
Ben Johnson (12) 30
Rafal Slomkowski (12) 31
James Ackland (12) 32
Tom Cohen (11) 33
Todd Langham (12) 34
Sophie Smith (12) 35
Megan Johnson (11) 36
Loren Barnard (12) 37
Jacob Rudge (12) 38

Jordan Merritt (11) 39

Altwood CE School, Maidenhead
Renée Shaw (12) 39
Elisha King (12) 40
Awyis Hussain (13) 41
Bryony Akerman (13) 42
Heather Thompson (14) 43
Omar Mahmood (15) 44

Beaufort Community School, Tuffley
Lucy Whayman (12) 44
Ben Chamberlain (11) 45
Shannon Brown (13) 46
Edward Clapton (13) 48
Charlie Walker (12) 49
Benayak Karki (12) 50
Hannah Elliss (13) 51
Thomas Stevens (13) 52
Alana Turner (13) 53
Stephanie Karenga (12) 54
Charlotte Brain (13) 55
Chelsea Bryon (13) 56
Daniel Stewart (13) 57
Emma Philip (12) 58
Jordan Hutchinson (12) 59
Joshua Dowd (13) 60
Shannon Kelly (13) 61
Courtney Wood (12) 62
Courtney Hodges (13) 63
Kayleigh Andrews (12) 64
Sian Scarratt (13) 65
Georgia Sandford (13) 66
Leah Robinson (13) 67
Amy Balding (13) 68
Megan Reeves (12) 69
Taylor Sandford (13) 70
Jessica Crane (13) 71

Chelsea Burnham (12) 72
Lauren Louise Stroud (13) 73
Laura Beacham (12) 74
Steven Bevan (12) 75
Hannah Jones (13) 76
Daniela Valkova (11) 76
Owen Jones (11) 77
Timothy Reeves (12) 78
John Pemberton (11) 78
Jordan Lord (12) 79
Ryan Shepherd (12) 79
Craig Pierce (12) 80
Charlotte Bailes (12) 80
Dan Langley (12) 81
Harriet Fortey (12) 81
Rhiannon Eveleigh (12) 82
Kieran McDonagh (12) 82
Michelle Hodge (12) 83
Rebecca Lawrence (11) 83
Rebecca Riselli (12) 84
Amreet Kaur Atwal (12) 85

Challney High School for Girls, Luton
Tasmia Asif (12) 86
Kainaat Sheikh (12) 87
Almira Rafeeque (15) 88
Sabeera Dar (13) 89
Tasnima Ahmed (13) 90
Kiran Riaz (13) 91
Muneebah Bashrat (13) 92
Amina Rizvi (13) 93
Sehar Ahmad (12) 94
Simranpreet Kaur Summan (12) 95
Afeera Jamil (13) 96
Amna Tariq (13) 97

Churchdown School, Churchdown
Euan Jephcote (12) 97
Emily Garfield (13) 98
Edie Stone (12) 99
Nathan Evans (13) 100
Sam Pennington (13) 101

Amy-Jo Taylor (12) 102
Lauren Knight (12) 102
Bethan Heather Richards (13) 103
Jake Wolstencroft (12) 103
Ryan Harris (12) 104
Macauley Medcroft (13) 104
Cobi Ho (13) 105
Keeley Bishop (13) 105
Kefren Milne (13) 106
James Blackshaw Dobbins (11) 107
Alexander Hitchman (12) 107
Bethany Stevens (12) 108
Kelsey Webb (13) 109
Sam Mansell (12) 109
Peter Lee (14) 110
Gemma Dooley (12) 110
James Bourke (12) 111
Jess Waghorn (12) 111
Callum Dawson-Williams (11) 112
Lauren McLean (12) 112
Chloe-May Barton (13) 113
Henry Noble (12) 113
Alice Jones (12) 114

Cornwallis Academy, Maidstone
Daniel Bristow (12) 114
Katie Bishop (14) &
Amber Kirk (13) 115
Jazmin Qunta &
Kirsty Russell (14) 116
Bethany Carreras (12) 117
Jacob Andreassen (12) 117
Elaine Kemp (14) 118
Ellie Wyatt (12) 118
Jack French (12) 119
Angus Knowler (12) 119
Billie Allbury-Smith (12) 120
Lianna Wallace (13) 120
Laura Wells &
Amie Chattenton (14) 121
Charlotte Lavender (13) 121
Michael Welbourne (12) 122
Hannah Tyler (12) 122

Adam Shallcross (13) 123
Paige Souten (12) 123
Aimee Miller (12) 124
Gemma Lawrance (13)................... 124
Lauren Butler (12)........................... 125
Toby Patey-Ford 125
Emma Clark (14) 126
Molly Palmer (12) 126
Charlotte Pursey (12) 126
Charley Bray (11)............................ 127

Denefield School, Tilehurst
Rebecca Harding (14) 127
Shawni James Vickery (11) 128
Laura Szandrowycz (11)................. 128
Tobiasz Nadworny (12).................... 128
Samara Edwards (11)..................... 129

Heathfield Community College, Heathfield
Lucy Meilack (12) 129
Elly Ambridge (13) 130
Alex von Barnholt (13)..................... 131
Jessica Kraft (12)............................. 132
Sophie-Rose McDonagh (12).......... 134
Emily Simpson (13) 135
Leyla Owen (13).............................. 136
Skye Ostermeyer (13) 137
Jess Douglas (13)............................ 138

Highcrest Community School, High Wycombe
Richard Crawley (12)....................... 138
Darrian George-Johnson (12).......... 139
Xyla Jacobs (12).............................. 140
Caity Hicks (12) 141
Emma Prince (12)............................ 142
Charlotte Louise
Helene Lawrence (12) 143
Charlie Basham (12)........................ 144
Jeremiah Patel (11) 144
Olivia Sutherland (12)...................... 145
Dannii Laine (12).............................. 145

Holywells High School, Ipswich
Shannon Johnson (13) 146
Katie Chaplin (11)............................ 147
Shannon Sewell (13) 148
Chelsea Chatfield (12)..................... 149
Candice Sobers (11)........................ 150
Eloise Wells (13).............................. 151
Owen Lander (12)............................ 152
Ryan Allington (12) 153
Ellen Day (13).................................. 153
Onica Hussain (12).......................... 154
Chloe Wright (12) 154
Devon Old-Gooch (13) 155
Warren Curtis (12)........................... 155
Laura Bowen (13)............................ 156
Jack Podd (12) 156
Chloe Adams (12)............................ 157
Toni Maria Abrahams (12) 157
Rhiannon Culley (12)....................... 158
Ryan Shimmon (13)......................... 158
Sydney Lawson-Whitear (12).......... 159
Jordan Cook & Brad Goodchild (13) 159
Charlie Duric-Last (13) 160
Olivia Halsey (13) 160
Chloe Louise Bartrum (13) 161
Ben Aldous (12)............................... 161

Kemnal Technology College, Sidcup
Thomas Desborough (13)................ 162
Jack Carnell (12) 163
Connor Tompsett (12)...................... 163
Miles Taylor (13) 164
Michael Beven (12).......................... 164
Harry Stapley (13) 165
Jozef Szkoda (13)............................ 166
Max Turner Howard (13).................. 166

Leigh Technology College, Dartford
Aneghe Regina Onodjamue (13)..... 167

Marston Vale Middle School, Stewartby
Natalie Smith (12) 168
Shannon Gibson (12) 168
Eleanor Dunn (12) 169
Megan Rowe (12) 169
Emilia Bugg (12) 170
Ellie Bancroft-Blake (12) 170
Alex Keech (12) 171
Abigail Perrin (12) 171
Tia Harris (12) 172
Harriet Beacon (12) 172
Lucy Alexander (12) 173
Lauren Kirby (12) 173
Lowri Jones (12) 174
Leah Carter (13) 174
Rianna Clark (12) 175
Casey Page (13) 175
Rebecca Stanton (11) 176
Megan Creamer (11) 176
Holly Smith (12) 176

Putteridge High School, Luton
Mohammed Ibrar Ali Razaq (13) 177

Ranelagh School, Bracknell
Alice Cole (12) 177
Robert Dyster (12) 178
Rachel Lammin (13) 179
Madeleine Oliver (12) 180
Adam Chave-Jones (12) 181
Amy Butcher (12) 181
Georgina Wood (12) 182
Luke Seymour (12) 182
Maisie Turner (12) 183
Emily Wilson (12) 183
Sophie Adams (12) 184
Catherine Powell (12) 184
Naomi Koefman (12) 185
Alice Harvey (12) 185
Emma Sidey (11) 186
Blake Wilson (12) 186

Eleanor Nicolaides (12) 187
Will Norman (12) 187
Beth Carpenter (12) 188
James Cunningham (12) 188
Chloe Giles (12) 189
Frankie Overton Hatton (12) 189
Katie Scott (12) 190
Molly Greenfield (12) 190
Olivia Winter (12) 191
Eden Sinclair (11) 191
Josh Brown (11) 191
Euan Farrow (12) 192
James Moul (12) 192
Jack Leyland (12) 192

Sandhurst School, Sandhurst
Jessica Campbell (17) 193
Jack Day (16) 194
Emma-Louise Downe (13) 195
Bryony Ford (12) 195
Megan Humphrey (12) 196

Southend High School for Girls, Southend-on-Sea
Aimée Mundy (13) 196
Nancy Jones (13) 197
Jessica Allen (12) 198
Ayda Khanchi (13) 199
Rachele Anne Lewis (13) 200
Laura Felton-Hustwitt (13) 201
Abigail Kelly (13) 202
Isabella Wolfe (13) 203
Annabelle Abrahams (12) 204
Jessie Stack (13) 205
Alya Omar (12) 205
Millie Guy (13) 206
Paloma Sanz (13) 207
Lydia Prior (12) 207
Meredith Mills (13) 208
Laura Bettany (13) 208
Jemima Bouch (12) 209
Katie Webster (13) 209
Emily Muggleton (13) 210

Eunice Christine Otoo (13) 210
Amy Layzell (13) 211
Anna Price (11) 212
Ruby Yeomans (13) 213
Hannah Jones (13) 214
Maariya Arshad (13) 215

The Emmbrook School, Wokingham
Jasmine Tuson (12) 215
Kerys Meredew (12) 216
Chloe Moore (13) 217
Jordan Onraet-Wells (13) 218

The Leys School, Cambridge
William Parker (14) 218
Nicole Montague (13) 219
Harriet Prior (13) 221
Alexandra Gray (14) 221
Rory Purvis (13) 222
Jack Willmott (14) 222

The New Rush Hall School, Hainault
Sediqah-Jaye Thompson-Miller (14) 223

The Philip Morant School & College, Colchester
Molly Coker (12) 224

Woodlands School, Basildon
Larhys Skidmore (12) 225
Alex Ronnie Alan Nicholson (12) 225
Richard Langton (12) 226
Cacey-Jayne Cox (12) 226
Keith King (11) 227
Ashton Thomas Silk (11) 227

The Poems

Me And My Mum

Me and my mum were getting on fine,
Till one day she came to mine,
She was crying, she'd had a fight,
She had pretended to kill me on sight,
I was scared and upset, I didn't know what to do,
So I had counselling and now I am cool,
Now I am fine and up to no good,
Well, that's me, I'm a kid
So what are you going to do?

Kenny Izatt (13)

Saturday Night

Lately I've been lost.

My mind wanders between monotony
And futility.

Every day contains only a slight variation on the events of the previous,
And the voices of dead philosophers are ever so keen to remind me that there is, indeed, 'more to life'.

My room has four walls.
It is sparse. Spartan, as it could be described . . .

Physical boundaries, however, mean very little.
As far as I am concerned,

it is a universe of thought.

Amidst this rugged, charming, alarming, unexplored, ultimately
Apathetic universe . . .
a child wanders.

Scientifically, it is referred to as 'dendritic branching'.

Metaphorically? War.

An unlikely couple, the world of Monotony and the spirit of Ennui have spawned the child known as Thought.

Thought is dangerous,
nefarious,
forever bent on freedom,

as it wages an eternal war against Futility
in the unexplored universe.

At zero gravity, the stars explode -
and burn feverishly,
only to eventually die out after a life of no acknowledgement
and heavy contemplation.

Futility is the murderer.
Married to Patience.

Generously,
Futility allows these stars to shine until the end,
until they may be reborn again.

Always, he is the victor.

Thought and Futility meet -
mid-air.

They are the bullets,
they are the missiles,
they are the fired off neurones,
in my so very human brain.

A war in space: they collide.

But,
deprived of oxygen,
they are deprived of their rightful place
as brilliant,
magnificent,
fiery explosions.

Gracefully, these brethren descend -
into the cemetery of unused thoughts . . .
only to be borne anew.

The process is relentless.
The process, I am told, is called 'puberty'.

I am apt, however, to disbelieve this, and characterise this universal war;
comprised of a thousand tiny conflicts . . .
as solely mine.

Rebecca Thomas

The Ballad the Sunken Yacht

A family of four
two daughters, their mum and dad
On 27th April
sank their family yacht.
Oh why? Oh why?

They were rescued by
the crew of HMS Clyde
they were only 200 miles away
and arrived in a day.
Oh why? Oh why?

Thankfully they were uninjured
but the yacht
was no more.
Oh why? Oh why?

They had been sailing
since March 2007
they had just left
the port of Georgia, USA.
Oh why? Oh why?

They were heading
to South Africa
when they hit a
low-lying iceberg.
Oh why? Oh why?

The iceberg is known
as a 'growler'
and is similar to
what the Titanic hit.
Oh why? Oh why?

When the iceberg struck
the 60ft yacht took on
water and suffered
an engine failure.
Oh why? Oh why?

The poor yacht

the hull was undamaged
though the inside
was wrecked and destroyed.
Oh why? Oh why?

In the village they came from
they were rarely seen
the pub landlord said
they called themselves Lord and Lady
Oh why? Oh why?

This ballad tells a story
be careful when you sail
in a big yacht
and say you are a Lord or Lady!
Oh why? Oh why?

Matt Grimston (12)
Aldworth Science College, Basingstoke

Fishy Thief

A man got dressed and went to sea
He wondered and pondered on how his day would be,
With him he took his camera and spear,
It was a glorious day and he had no fear.

Jack climbed down the ladder of his boat,
A gust of wind got stuck in his throat,
Jack entered the sea, it was very cold,
There was no going back, he just had to be bold.

He went to film something in the deep blue sea,
He swam around and around, it was nice to be free,
He swam around without any fear,
When he turned around, the octopus was there.

To Jack's shock and total surprise,
The octopus looked him straight in his eyes,
The octopus with his tentacle stretched out wide,
Stole his camera and went off to hide!

Jamie Young (11)
Aldworth Science College, Basingstoke

The Ballad Of Princess Diana

Princess Diana, so sweet,
So young, life just seemed a blur.
In sunny days, she saw her prince,
She loved him; he loved her.

Charles, Prince of Wales,
It was said he loved another,
A very strange relationship,
Yet Diana, he still loved her!

But the romance wasn't meant to last,
And soon it fell apart,
A man called Dodi came along,
And fixed her broken heart.

She fell in love, for the last time,
Soon they were to be wed,
With pictures in the media,
And romance in the bed.

The media went crazy,
Pictures on every page,
And when the nation loved it,
The royals were in rage!

The publication of their love,
Put pressure on the Queen,
Someone asked a question,
And she wanted to scream!

But luckily for her,
A mere coincidence,
For the gracious young Diana,
An accident unable to sense.

A trip to Paris in France,
Was a great mistake,
For on that night, she and her lover,
Were going on a break.

But it turned out,
Like no one would have wanted,
The car, it crashed,
And now the car is haunted!

Where are you now Diana?
Your heart is so pure,
Did it hurt you in the car
As you fell through the car door?

For poor Diana died,
On the dreadful night,
Doctors tried for two whole hours,
To save her in her fight.

From now on, it will be known,
That August 31st 1997,
Was the day that Princess Diana,
Drifted up to Heaven.

Rhiannon Michelle Taylor (12)
Aldworth Science College, Basingstoke

War

People running, screaming out loud,
The sound of guns is a piercing sound.
Now there are bodies on the ground,
Are wars something of which to be proud?

Guns and bullets lined up in a row,
'Move out the way!' shouted my friend Joe.
Now there are bodies on the ground,
Are wars something of which to be proud?

There are lots of tanks moving fastly,
The sight of blood - is it ghastly?
Now there are bodies on the ground,
Are wars something of which to be proud?

One by one soldiers return home,
Some soldiers are missing, does anybody know?
Now there are bodies on the ground,
Are wars something of which to be proud?

Lucy Peters (11)
Aldworth Science College, Basingstoke

Ballad Of Scribblenauts

One fine day at E3
Everyone was filled with glee
Because a new game was revealed
It had many things you could wield

That game, 'Scribblenauts', had many nouns
And no one there had a frown
But unfortunately they were wrong
They were wrong by very long

People tried but the game couldn't break
Everyone thought it was amazingly great
No one ever seemed to notice
That parts of the game were atrocious

Soon the game was released
But, alas, it was a beast
People played it but then
The controls handled like a slippery hen

The camera was also bad
It made no one glad
It only stayed for a couple of seconds
It was wrong everyone reckoned

It won the biggest disappointment award
And for it no one did applaud
It could have easily been a gem
'But it was deficient' said the men.

'How could this happen?' the makers said
'We went for days with no bed
We thought we'd made an exemplary breakthrough
Oh whatever shall we do?'

'Make a sequel,' the public said
'But the first was great,' said various blockheads
Back in the office the makers thought
'That's what we'll do to get more than a nought.

It will take a while but it will be worth it
This time we'll use more of our wit
We'll add d-pad control and adjectives too
And loads of upright words to begin anew.'

'Yes!' the public cried
'By the end of this our hopes won't have died
This game will be fantastic
It might even be a classic.'

As of now the game's yet to be released
When will it finally be unleashed?
Will they finally get it right . . .
Or will people hate it day and night?

Elliott Kerwick (12)
Aldworth Science College, Basingstoke

Asian Hornets

If you are nervous around stinging insects,
You might think bees are bad
And hornets are annoying pests.
They can drive you mad.

The unpleasant little critters.

Well you ain't seen nothing yet!
A new hornet's on the way
To put our native breed to shame.
It is acclaimed from the Middle East.

The unpleasant little critters.

They've come to kill our bees.
There is no way of controlling the spread.
The firefighters try their best to keep
The bees from their deathbed.

The unpleasant little critters.

Humans have been attacked too.
They're coming two by two.
They feed the bees to their young.

The unpleasant little critters.

Oliver Sayer (12)
Aldworth Science College, Basingstoke

The Ballad Of Helen Skelton

It was spring 2010
When Helen Skelton met the Amazon River,
Indeed, she was brave,
And she certainly didn't dither.

The Amazon awaited her,
Its meanders long and winding,
Melted into the horizon,
The nature simply blinding!

She did it for the children,
She did it for Sports Relief,
She did it despite the hardship,
For she had much belief.

The journey it did take her
Six long sweltering weeks,
Through the terrible weather,
Which forever remained so bleak.

The experts told her she would fail,
For she was the first woman to do it,
But even after her training,
She deserved the credit.

Her co-presenters stuck up for her,
They didn't want to let her down,
They didn't want to let her go,
If she was going to drown.

She found it hard,
She found it tough,
All because of the river,
Which was forever so very rough.

Her little boat,
Such a beautiful red,
It helped her down the river,
But it wasn't exactly a bed.

Then, after six long weeks,
She made it to the finish line,
Just inside Brazil,
And the weather was just sublime!

'I may be used to creating,
But for those who were against me,
This will be a blow,
Because now look what they see.'

So, this story goes to show,
That life can be as good as paradise,
Even as good as gold,
Even if you don't follow all the experts' advice.

Daniel Reid (12)
Aldworth Science College, Basingstoke

The Ballad Of The Adopting Hen

A broody hen in Shropshire
Has adopted a litter of puppies,
She's literally taken them under her wing
Without the help of her hubbies.

When the little pups' mother, Nettle,
Left to go for a prowl,
Mabel, the hen, who lived in the house,
Approached them with a sly but friendly scowl.

To say that Nettle was angry
Would be putting it very mild,
Let's just say she was a bit shocked . . .
Oh, what am I saying? She went wild!

But after a while Nettle calmed down,
And they each took it in turns
To look after the little brown and cute fluff bags
And give them the attention the pups hadn't earned.

So here it is everyone,
A true story that surprised you all
To think that a hen would 'adopt' another animal,
So brown, furry and small!

Elsa Anderson
Aldworth Science College, Basingstoke

The Ballad Of The Piece Of Paper

Lyrics can tell a story,
like 'A Day in the Life',
or they can tell a story
about troubles with the wife.

On this piece of paper,
these things are oh, so true.
From feelings of despair,
to days of feeling blue.

These awesome lyrics
are going 'under the hammer'
in a week or two -
so write it in your planner!

The lyrics going on sale,
were written by John Lennon.
He spelt 'film' 'flim'
oh, he was a lemon!

With its languorous cry
of 'I'd love to turn you on',
it actually has a meaning -
his marriage was going wrong.

This sheet of lyrics,
is worth a lot of money.
Whoever spends that much,
must be kind of funny.

This song, 'A Day in the Life',
based on the news articles,
inspired by the headlines,
supplied by boys on bicycles.

As we have established,
this song is going on sale.
It was sung by The Beatles,
who everyone did hail.

On this piece of paper
this song is rather sad
but despite this little detail,
the song isn't that bad!

Lyrics can tell a story
like 'A Day in the Life',
or they can tell a story
about troubles with the wife.

On this piece of paper,
these things are oh, so true.
From feelings of despair,
to days of feeling blue.

Lauren Wiltshire (12)
Aldworth Science College, Basingstoke

Tony Blair Lost His Job

In 2007, Tony Blair went down
And lost his job to Gordon Brown
He gave up living at Number Ten
He lost his job and all his men

Tony Blair didn't put up a fight
So Gordon Brown saw the sight
He gave up living at Number Ten
He lost his job and all his men

Gordon Brown grabbed his chance
Tony Blair didn't give it another glance
He gave up living at Number Ten
He lost his job and all his men

Gordon Brown was so tight
He made us pay more for our electric and light
He gave up living at Number Ten
He lost his job and all his men

In 2007, Tony Blair went down
And lost his job to Gordon Brown
He gave up living at Number Ten
He lost his job and all his men.

Harlie-Jaine Rolfe (12)
Aldworth Science College, Basingstoke

The Ballad Of Madeleine McCann

A holiday in Portugal
For Kate and Gerry McCann
Would they've gone if they'd known
That their holiday would not go to plan?

Their daughter, she was stolen,
Disappeared without a trace,
Poor, defenceless Madeleine,
Whose parents had lost
Something impossible to replace.

Madeleine had vanished,
Without anyone to blame,
One thing was certain,
Life would never be the same.

All around the world,
Sightings popped up, whether or not in the head,
Of poor little Madeleine McCann,
Unfortunately these herrings turned out to be red.

Nobody could imagine who was behind it,
So the parents were named as suspects,
Whether or not this was fair,
This was impossible to expect.

Luckily this status was lifted,
Off Kate and Gerry McCann,
Who were allowed to fly back home,
It seems their holiday hadn't gone to plan.

Think of their grief,
Their terrible sorrow,
Like a mournful hole blown through their life,
A part that was impossible to regrow.

How could this have happened
For someone to vanish off the system?
And leave in her wake the shattered lives of many
in the wake of this merciless phantom?

Madeleine McCann, the poor defenceless soul,
Stolen from her family
And her friends of old.
She was dropped from the world we know, awfully.

A holiday in Portugal,
For Kate and Gerry McCann,
Would they've gone if they had known,
That their holiday wouldn't go to plan?

Ben Cossar (11)
Aldworth Science College, Basingstoke

The Ballad Of Ruben

The plane flew straight downwards
One hundred and three people died
The plane crumpled on the ground
There one boy lay, luckily he was alive.

The boy in the hospital bed
All wires going through him
He had a really sore head
He then got wheeled away

The family came rushing around the corner
With sadness on their faces
Everyone was relieved and happy
The nephew smiled a cheeky smile back at them

They stayed with him using an oxygen mask
He used the mask to keep him alive
For that, everyone sighed
On that day everyone cried

That day was one of the saddest ever
No one knows why the aeroplane went down
It is still a conspiracy how it happened
But when I think, I frown.

Bradley Lambell (12)
Aldworth Science College, Basingstoke

The Ballad Of Madeleine McCann

On the 3rd May 2007
From the centre of Praia da Luz
Madeleine McCann, her face so golden,
Was taken from the ones she loved.

Where are you Madeline?
Where have you gone?
Sweet baby Madeleine,
Our little swan.

Her two baby twins Sean and Amelie,
Miss her so much,
The Devil stole the angel they loved
And their broken hearts they clutch.

Where are you Madeline?
Where have you gone?
Sweet baby Madeleine,
Our little swan.

And at the end of May they went away
To receive their blessing from the Pope.
And the desperation within their hearts
Sent them to the police, their only hope.

Where are you Madeline?
Where have you gone?
Sweet baby Madeleine,
Our little swan.

And a woman that loved Madeleine
Who was actually using it for drugs
Claimed to be raising money
And was jailed for three months.

Where are you Madeline?
Where have you gone?
Sweet baby Madeleine,
Our little swan.

On the 10th August, 100 days
Madeleine was declared found.
Her parents' hearts rose with joy but . . .
It was an ordinary child, not Madeleine,
Their hearts sank again.

Where are you Madeleine?
Where have you gone?
We thought we'd found you,
Our dear little swan.

Heidi Padoin (12)
Aldworth Science College, Basingstoke

The Ballad Of Ruben

The plane was falling towards the Earth
The blood flew everywhere
Worst tragedy ever
Nobody seemed to care

A little boy called Ruben Van Assouw
He was perfect
He never told a lie
Why should his family die?

There was only one survivor
Ruben was his name
We found him on a cliff edge
And there he lay in pain

The crash was on the headlines
Everyone was watching
The crash was from a high altitude
It looked like he had been boxing

He had got tubes all over him
Because he was in hospital
His family stayed to comfort him
His family prayed the gospel.

George Jones
Aldworth Science College, Basingstoke

The Ballad Of The 20 Minute Coaster Terror

On a sunny 5th of May,
In a happy 2010,
An incident happened
To two thrill-seeking men.

On an expensive Mumbo Jumbo ride,
In a fun Flamingo Land,
Malton, in North Yorks, near the beach it is,
So on their feet some people had sand.

There was a water ride,
A poncho one had to wear.
It got stuck in the mechanism,
It gave them quite a scare.

They held on tight as the ride
Stopped and left them hanging
Upside down, 50ft in the air,
For 20 minutes they heard a lot of clanging.

They were helped down,
From the £4 million ride,
After staff released them
Who were on their side.

The manager announced,
'The ride doesn't have a fault,
It was just a poncho from one of the guests,
Their other poncho is in the boot of his Renault!'

In eyewitness interview revealed,
'There was quite a big crowd,
And everyone was worried for the men,
But I must say the commotion was very loud.'

After the two men were out,
'We were so scared
And all the blood rushed to our heads,'
This they declared.

From that day the Mumbo Jumbo ride
Has been working perfectly,
It had some maintenance
And now not a bit works badly.

So on a sunny 5th May,
In a happy 2010,
An incident happened,
To two thrill-seeking men.

Daniel Goodenough (12)
Aldworth Science College, Basingstoke

The Plane Crash

The people came on the plane
Worried about nothing, not even pain
Hundreds died
They didn't even try

The plane took off into the air
Over the lake, over the fair
Hundreds died
And they didn't even try

They heard a noise from the engine
When they saw a pigeon
Hundreds died
And they didn't try

The plane started falling from the night sky
After they went over West High
Hundreds died
And they didn't even try

It almost hit the ground
Everyone was silent, not even a sound
Hundreds died
And they didn't even try

There was an explosion
Everyone could hear the mighty implosion
Hundreds died
And they didn't even try.

Ryan Parker (12)
Aldworth Science College, Basingstoke

The Ballad Of The Supercar

A vintage Bugatti Supercar
Sold about a week ago
To a museum in California
To go on public show

It was for 30 million dollars
Or 20 million pounds
What an expensive automobile
The most expensive in the world.

The car is very romantic
Very old-fashioned and posh
It's a car from the 1930s
I think it'll need a wash.

The car is a grey-blue colour
The windows - very small
The wheels are tiny rubber things
With no suspension at all!

The 57SC Atlantic
Is the name of the model
It is really quite fantastic
But driving it isn't a doddle!

Even though the car is very old now
Seventy-six years to be precise
The car is an antique now.
So you better roll the dice.

The rich guy was Dr Williamson
Who bought the historic car
He bought it at an auction
The price though - how bizarre!

It doesn't have a V8 engine
It doesn't have a sat nav
It does, though, have a specific design
A French Deco Blue to be exact.

I love this car, I really do
Although it's not the latest.
I love this car, I really do

I think it's just the greatest.

A Vintage Bugatti supercar
Sold about a week ago
To a museum in California
To go on public show.

Musa Ahmad (11)
Aldworth Science College, Basingstoke

The Ballad Of Ruben

The plane, it flew straight downwards
A hundred and three people died
The plane crashed into the ground
On the ground they lay

The boy was in hospital in bed
Breathing through an oxygen mask
The boy didn't know about his family
The hospital staff did their task

This was the darkest day in history
They couldn't save all the passengers
The crash was a mystery
He was lying in the crash with broken legs

There was a boy survivor
Ruben was his name
We found him on the cliff edge
And there he lay in pain

The crash was in the headlines
Everybody was watching
There was a deadline
Everyone was crying

They were praying for him
They could cry no more
He was very limp
Their eyes were dry.

Ollie Shaw (12)
Aldworth Science College, Basingstoke

The Ballad Of Young Love Blossoms At Hogwarts!

Love is the essence of nature,
Love is the key to peace,
Love cannot be bought, only stolen or earned,
But never will love cease.

Little Ginny and Gellert,
Young Bonnie and Jamie,
Their vows state, even in the darkest place,
They are together running free.

It coils around her finger's end,
Shimmering bright in silver sterling,
A loving token of their wondrous bond,
Otherwise known as an engagement ring.

It dives deep inside her soul,
The magic of true romance,
But such a colossal step, at the age of 19.
Have they got any chance?

They say their home is Hogwarts,
Of where they play their parts,
No matter how far, they desperately reach out,
To a passion beyond their hearts.

Zoe, her name, sweet Zoe,
A love that once Jamie lost sight,
A reflection of memories bounce back to haunt,
Resemblance of dear Bonnie Wright.

Like a twisting and turning roller coaster,
Time flies when love is deep,
At the end of the ride a new journey begins,
Six months of life you promise to keep.

Flamed hair rests upon her head,
Matches her pale bleached face,
You can see why in fact their hearts stay intact,
Did beauty only solve this case?

They say Jamie is a gift to acting,
They say Bonnie is tender and young,
But uncertainly revealed to the press' eyes,
But still serenade is sung.

Love is the essence of nature,
Love is the key to peace,
Love cannot be bought, only stolen or earned,
But never will love cease!

Isabelle Kersley (12)
Aldworth Science College, Basingstoke

The Ballad Of Ruben

Why did 103 die
All because of one big crash?
So many people died needlessly
Could it be the volcanic ash?

The only survivor, Ruben, a boy
Of only eight, such a mistake
Now he has no family to enjoy
What he wants will have to wait

Now he is lying in a bed
With loads of machines all around
He's hurt his head
All he wants is to see his mum

'Mum, Dad,' poor Ruben shouts
But they are no longer here
The hideous truth he has to black out
His life is ruined

As an orphan his life will be hell
No mother, no father, no brother
We surely feel sorry for him
He will never be an ordinary boy like any other.

Courtney Edenbrow (12)
Aldworth Science College, Basingstoke

The Ballad Of Hairstyle

If you perfect the way of hair
the soft and wavy look
everybody will stop and stare
as that amazing look has now been took

Straight and sleek is very out
as everyone should know
if people don't stop and shout
the fact will surely show

'How do I get this awesome fashion?'
asked someone without a comb
'It's all about the flaring passion
and it's easy to achieve at home!'

So the hair to wear is nice soft waves
and body for ruffled effects
this is the look to wear to raves
and I don't know anyone who objects

Your hair should be below your shoulders
to avoid looking like a mushroom
it should not go hard like boulders
and you should never just assume.

You should always use some kind of spray
for that extra protection
your roots are especially vulnerable in May
so make the right selection.

If you want that professional finish
you'll need a good round brush
that way your hair won't diminish
and it will look ultra-lush.

When you blow-dry your luscious hair
you will need some clips
else you'll get quite a scare
when finding some nasty blips

When you take out your magical rollers
remember to remove vertically
a corkscrew motion will attract many actors
and give you a soft spiral very slickly.

Now it's time to loosen your curls
and make them into soft waves
run your fingers through to unfurl
the style that everyone craves!

Amber Burton (12)
Aldworth Science College, Basingstoke

Volcanic Eruption

Volcanic eruption
Causing destruction
Nothing like burning heat
For all of us to defeat

Run and hide
Waiting until it has died
Running and screaming is not fun
Loud noises of disruption

Wherever we go it will follow
Leaving a trail of sadness and sorrow
Soon in the news then world-wide
Waiting until somebody arrives

Smoke goes up in the sky
Blocking the path of planes that fly
People stranded on their holidays
Willing to go back any day.

Crushing everything that gets in its way
Until it has had enough of the day
It goes back to where it lay
Waiting to erupt another day.

Rabin Magar (12)
Aldworth Science College, Basingstoke

The Ballad Of Bournemouth Bees

In a place far away,
Not in Portsmouth,
On a Wednesday,
Somewhere near Bournemouth.

There was a cloud
Of black and yellow bees,
There was a sound
Like the buzz of 1000 PCs.

To get through them you had to kick,
As well as that you could punch,
Find your bee and take your pick,
And you might just earn your lunch!

You could lock the door,
To stop them entering your house,
So you wouldn't stand in awe,
As they killed your pet mouse!

You could also shut the windows
To stop the intruding insects,
So they didn't dispose
Their stuff on your beds!

Even after hours
Of frustration,
Bees still covered flowers,
Near Bournemouth station.

When the swarm had moved on,
Lots of dead bees remained,
It hit the people like a bomb,
That the place would never be the same.

To us bees are vital,
To plants they are as well,
We lost a grand total,
It was like falling down a well.

Bees do something called pollination,
They do it on crops and flowers,
Without them there would be no nation,
Therefore they have wondrous powers!

Hundreds and hundreds of bees were killed,
Being run over by cars,
The bee colony we must rebuild,
And we have to do it fast!

Robert Scott (11)
Aldworth Science College, Basingstoke

Michael Jackson

Michael Jackson, king of pop,
There you sang and danced and would never stop,
Your doctor made a mistake,
By giving you things you shouldn't take.

Michael Jackson, you were the best,
Until you died, you didn't care less,
Your doctor made a mistake,
By giving you things you shouldn't take.

Michael Jackson, you were so brave,
Unfortunately now you're in a grave,
Your doctor made a mistake,
By giving you things you shouldn't take.

Michael Jackson, now you're gone,
We're sad, but we have got to carry on,
Your doctor made a mistake,
By giving you things you shouldn't take.

Michael Jackson, you were number one,
Top of the charts, you may have won,
Your doctor made a mistake,
By giving you things you shouldn't take.

Brian Radwell (12)
Aldworth Science College, Basingstoke

Ballad Of A Hero

Gerrard is his name.
Football is his game.
Gerrard, Gerrard.

With Torres out hurt,
Relegation is a cert.
Gerrard, Gerrard.

Twelve he's already scored.
As the crowd roared.
Gerrard, Gerrard.

His 2003 League Cup belter was the best.
As he celebrated in only his vest.
Gerrard, Gerrard.

A game against Olympia that ended one-nil.
A 25-yard stunner leaves Gerrard the hero still.
Gerrard, Gerrard.

It was the greatest comeback the world has ever seen.
To come from 3-0 down against Milan, it was pretty mean.
Gerrard, Gerrard.

In 2006 it was West Ham.
But all I can say is Gerrard was the man.
Gerrard, Gerrard.

Then against Marseilles in 2008.
He tamed them with a stunner late.
Gerrard, Gerrard.

But when last season came,
It left Gerrard in the fame.
Gerrard, Gerrard.

So when next season comes,
Let's hope we don't feel glum.
Gerrard, Gerrard.

So Gerrard is his name.
Football is his game.
Gerrard, Gerrard.

Thomas Gammell (12)
Aldworth Science College, Basingstoke

Jade Goody Was Very Brave

A woman called Jade Goody had two kids,
and maybe she told some fibs.
But Jade Goody was very brave,
and all she had was her life to save.

Jade Goody found out she had cancer,
but unfortunately there wasn't an answer.
But Jade Goody was very brave,
and all she had was her life to save.

Jade Goody got engaged,
and it was probably the best decision she ever made.
But Jade Goody was very brave,
and all she had was her life to save.

Jade Goody then got married to a man called Jack,
and that is a well-known fact.
But Jade Goody was very brave,
and all she had was her life to save.

Unfortunately Jade Goody passed away
two months before the 22nd of May.
But Jade Goody was very brave,
and all she had was her life to save.

Bethany Stevens (12)
Aldworth Science College, Basingstoke

My Ballad - Ash

On a peaceful day
Just near a bay
A volcano erupted ash
And many on holiday lost a lot of cash

The ash was as light as dust
And all the aircraft companies were going to go bust
A volcano erupted ash
And many on holiday lost a lot of cash

People who are on holiday
Are stuck for more than a day
A volcano erupted ash
And many on holiday lost a lot of cash

The cloud sweeps in from Iceland
The weather has not gone as planned
A volcano erupted ash
And many on holiday lost a lot of cash

On the last day the air cleared
And a lot of people cheered
A volcano erupted ash
And many on holiday lost a lot of cash

Ben Johnson (12)
Aldworth Science College, Basingstoke

Chelsea Won The Title
But They Are Still Rubbish

Chelsea hit eight to win the title
For them it was vital
But I support Liverpool
Because Chelsea aren't cool

To win against Chelsea, Wigan failed
So they got nailed
But I support Liverpool
Because Chelsea aren't cool

Wigan were defeated
They got badly treated
But I support Liverpool
Because Chelsea aren't cool

Liverpool is the best
I'm proud to wear their crest on my chest
They should have won the title
And the Europa League, for us it was vital.

Rafal Slomkowski (12)
Aldworth Science College, Basingstoke

Election Ballad Poem

Gordon Brown,
he let me down,
now we need a new prime minister,
that isn't so sinister.

Is it going to be the Conservatives,
who might bring back preservatives?
Is it going to be the Liberal Democrats
who probably aren't that democratic?

Is it going to be Labour
whose odds aren't in their favour?
We need someone who takes us seriously,
who doesn't reply, 'Really?'

Oh!

Gordon Brown,
he let me down,
now we need a new prime minister,
that isn't so sinister.

James Ackland (12)
Aldworth Science College, Basingstoke

The Ash Cloud

The day began
The world awoke
All at once
There was a cloud of smoke

The planes were grounded
The people were stuck
Left at the airport
What bad luck

The coaches came
And left again
Taking people home
Women, children and men.

Then as fast as it came
It had gone once more
Costing us millions
And causing an uproar!

Tom Cohen (11)
Aldworth Science College, Basingstoke

The Volcano

The volcano grumbled and growled,
All you saw was a crowd,
They watched the smoke and fire,
As it flew higher and higher.

The smoke and ashes went through the sky . . .
And that's when people started to cry,
'We can't get home,
And all we have is a mobile phone.'

The airplanes had stopped,
And there was no more food in the shops,
Everyone's bellies were grumbling and growling
And then people started frowning.

They didn't know what to do,
And all they had to eat was baby goo,
Two weeks later the ash went away,
And the planes flew through the day.

Todd Langham (12)
Aldworth Science College, Basingstoke

Jade Goody

Jade Goody you were so brave
Your lovely sons you had to save
There you sat in a lot of pain
Trying to figure out, what's the aim?

Although it was hard
Everyone sent get well cards
There you sat in a lot of pain
Trying to figure out, what's the aim?

You had two boys
Who had a lot of joys
There you sat in a lot of pain
Trying to figure out, what's the aim?

You had a wonderful husband named Jack
Who would never lack
There you sat in a lot of pain
Trying to figure out, what's the aim?

Sophie Smith (12)
Aldworth Science College, Basingstoke

The Longest Night (Haiti Earthquake)

Crashing! Screaming! Am I dreaming?
A huge great crack has appeared in my ceiling!
People's voices all around,
Crying is the only sound.

Slipping! Sliding! The walls colliding!
I don't like the place where I'm hiding.
Trapped, cold, dark and dusty,
The smells around me are damp and musty.

Hungry! Thirsty! Nothing to see!
How long will I be here? When will they find me?
My leg is stuck! I can't get out!
What I must do is scream and shout!

The screaming and shouting has finally worked!
I saw my mum from beneath the dirt,
She pulled me out by the scruff of my jacket,
I can't believe she heard me over all that racket!

Megan Johnson (11)
Aldworth Science College, Basingstoke

Jade Goody

Jade Goody, you have made a wave
But being so big and really brave
You made everyone happy with your smile
You had trouble but you lived a while.

Jade Goody, we watched you in pain
But that was because you were not vain
Cancer, that's what took your life
Just after you became Jack's wife.

Jade Goody, now you've gone
We all have to carry on
You were missed much
And our hearts were touched.

Jade Goody, the Lord Christ, has tried so hard
So has everybody by sending you a card
Your boys and Jack were very sad
But when you went they went very mad.

Loren Barnard (12)
Aldworth Science College, Basingstoke

Volcanic Ash Cloud

The day awoke
The smell of smoke
Flights stopped
People stropped

Volcanic ash flew around
People's flights on the ground
Everyone was stuck in one place
That's what they all had to face

Engines roared
Children bored
No one was leaving
Airports heaving

A little bit of ash
Can it cause a plane to crash?
What's all the fuss?
We take a bus!

Jacob Rudge (12)
Aldworth Science College, Basingstoke

My Squirrel Poem

In the trees animals wait,
Until the clock reads five or eight.
When there's no children out to play,
The squirrels appear, it's that time of day.

At 12 o'clock, it's time for lunch,
It's nuts again, munch, munch, munch.
Bellies full, energy high,
Let's find our friends, fly, fly, fly.

We're at the park, winding down,
When shrieks of laughter are heard all around,
Screaming children having fun,
We join the queue, run, run, run.

Up and down, round and round,
We've having fun but now we're done.

Jordan Merritt (11)
Aldworth Science College, Basingstoke

It's Nature I Tell You, Nature

The grass below and the trees up high,
It's nature I tell you, nature!
The fish in the sea and the waters they swim,
It's nature I tell you, nature!
The weather, the sun, the moon also!
It's nature I tell you, nature!
The people on the streets, the dogs and cats they walk,
It's nature I tell you, nature!
The Earth, planets! The whole solar system!
It's nature I tell you, nature!
So what's not nature, you may ask?
Well clothes, houses, oh, and computers too!
And things like that, are all man made.
The rest is nature, I tell you, nature!

Renée Shaw (12)
Altwood CE School, Maidenhead

I Look Into The Mirror

I look into the mirror,
I don't see what you see,
No, none of you people will ever know the real me.

I look into the mirror,
I look behind the smile,
My blue eyes look even smaller, because I've been crying
for a while.

I look into the mirror,
I look behind the eyes,
Because when I'm all alone the bright happiness dies.

I look into the mirror,
I look behind the body,
My bones and heart are crushed, because of the things
that have been done to me.

I look into the mirror,
I look behind the heart,
You will never know what's happened to me,
inside I'm torn apart.

I look into the mirror,
I look behind my grit,
But walk a mile in my shoes, and try to understand it.

I look into the mirror,
Behind all the harsh remarks,
The 'sort your teeth out' and 'do something with your purple skin',
well I'm a different me at heart.

I look into the mirror,
I look behind the skin,
You will never see the bruises, the bruises I have within.

I look into the mirror,
I look behind the lies,
I think of the past and it brings tears to my eyes.

I look into the mirror,
I look behind the voice,
What's happened to me has happened, it wasn't my choice.

I look into the mirror,
I look behind the mind,
Go on, look for the real me, and see what you can find.

I look into the mirror,
Then I look at you,
Sitting there, not knowing the stuff that I've been through.

So look into the mirror,
Try being me,
Maybe I am more than just what you see.

Elisha King (12)
Altwood CE School, Maidenhead

Who And What Am I . . . ?

Who am I under this skin?
What am I under this grin?
Am I the old lady across the street
or am I the head I don't like to meet?
Who am I? What am I . . . ?

Am I my ex-boy Billy
or BFF Beth?
My great Aunt Lilly
or rich girl Jess?
Who am I? What am I . . . ?

Am I the primrose in the garden
or the vines in the shed?
Am I a fresh lush green
or bloodshot-red?
Who am I? What am I . . . ?

Am I the big bright moon
glowing not shining?
Or am I the dress in the store
full of gold lining?
Who am I under this skin?
What am I under this grin?

Awyis Hussain (13)
Altwood CE School, Maidenhead

I Miss You . . .

I look to the sky this very night
and a tear gently falls,
I think I'm going crazy,
when I hear those sweet soft calls
calling my name and beckoning me . . .

I close my eyes and your face I see.
What has gone wrong?
I'm not drunk
I'm not dying
but I cannot stop this endless crying . . .

I wish to see you
but you're no longer around,
apart from my crying, there isn't a sound.

Oh stop this madness!
It's killing me!
But I would die for you
you see

because you are my light
my handsome saviour
and I must stop this foolish behaviour.

Bryony Akerman (13)
Altwood CE School, Maidenhead

Twilight

A milky glow leaks into my blurred vision
Sat outside in this warm air, thinking of nature.
To be one with it, to join it.
A single breeze lifts my hair, infusing it with the mysteries
Sweet earth beholds, I listen to the outside chorus.
The peacefulness. The quietness
And then I stop. I wish not to break the approaching twilight
which I am encased in.
The coolness washes over me and my thoughts now are empty.
My mind, an emptiness waiting to be filled again
with the luxury of nature.
I weave more questions as this twilight is spreading
How can such beauty be painted onto a world.
Tainted with the hatred Man has caused?
Yet, somehow, I feel it fits.
Nature, so beautiful, so wonderful.
Sat in this twilight, I wish to know the answer.

Heather Thompson (14)
Altwood CE School, Maidenhead

A Drop Of Blood

This rotating orb whirls, endlessly
on one side hearts are fusing in a deathless flame
but as this spherical object spins,
hearts are being burnt to a crisp
not in a fire of love but a combustion of hatred

A drop of blood
celebration or pain
the crimson elixir flowing into an empty chalice
or the scarlet solution
gushing out of a fatal wound

How do you interpret that rosy liquid?
do you see it as a romantic dinner accompanied by a bottle
of the finest red?
or do you see the ignition of gunpowder
causing a cartridge of ammunition
to penetrate the heart of an absent loved one?

Omar Mahmood (15)
Altwood CE School, Maidenhead

Winter Fun

Snow falling to the ground,
Children out playing,
On the hill sleighing.

Christmas trees arrive so bare,
Only to be dressed with lights,
By children having a snowball fight.

People having lots of fun,
Sledging down the hill,
And watching is the snowman standing very still.

People writing Christmas cards,
Whilst the presents lie under the tree,
Only to be opened by children full of glee.

Lucy Whayman (12)
Beaufort Community School, Tuffley

August

Warm weather finally arrives,
To brighten up your day,
Whilst children play.

While people relax,
and eat lots of snacks,
Around the pool.

Finally the day we've waited for,
A cake comes out in front,
I made a wish, it came true.

The last day of summer,
The day we hate the most,
An early night for me I think!

Ben Chamberlain (11)
Beaufort Community School, Tuffley

In The Woods

Blowing leaves
soil turmoil
wet dew clings
autumn's here
In the woods

Peeling bark
dark and deadly
crunching leaves
crushed by boots
In the woods

Birds fall silent
as the wind picks up
dark eyes gleaming
black aura glowing
As he walks in the woods

Wolves howling on the hills
far away they seem
black clouds rolling
as rain starts pouring
While he walks through the woods

His fine hair whips
behind his face
in bitter night air
stars above shimmer
While he walks in the woods

A petite wood hut
snuggled deep within trees
his deep voice booms
'Come out and see me!'
As he stands in the woods

The door creaks open
a slight girl appears
she smiles at the ground
he looks away.
As he watches her in the woods.

46

Her fair hair falls
upon her shoulders
shining like stars
and covers her face
As he watches the woods.

Choking back sobs
'Don't leave me again'
crystal tears fall
when she looks at him
And he looks away from her into the woods.

'I'm here to stay,'
he takes a step closer
and holds her gently
they both disappear
Into the woods.

Shannon Brown (13)
Beaufort Community School, Tuffley

Peleliu

Sat in the hull of a boat
feeling sick as it floats
light shining through the glass
thinking that I will never last
off to war we go.

Seeing as the door opens
hearing mortars hit the sea
smelling the sweat and blood
tasting the mist of the sea
off to war we go.

Coming off the boat
slicing through the sea
thinking of my children and me
from now on I can't flee
off to war we go.

As we get off our landing craft
and run at enemy fire
my comrades fall around me
they can hear the angels' choir
off to war we go.

There were no empty graves
so we left them in great caves
Death knocked hard on our door
but we didn't fall to the floor
off to war we go.

Our mission was made to be simple
but it was far from easy-peasy,
to storm the Peleliu airfield
but the enemy bases were sealed
off to war we go

We stopped the mortars
we took the field
we went to our quarters
we are the navy seals
off to war we go.

This was World War II
in the landing of Peleliu
off to war we go . . .

Edward Clapton (13)
Beaufort Community School, Tuffley

Rag Doll Adventure

As I sit here on the shelf
Keeley is nowhere to be seen
Then I spot her lying on the floor
She is messy and not a bit clean

This is my mission
Where my adventure starts
I grab my blanket
Covered in hearts.

I jump onto the bouncy bed
Tell Keeley, 'Don't worry, you're saved.'
We get back to the shelf
My hair is tangled and waved.

All the toys celebrate
And give me a great big clap
Then we see a toss from the bed
The girl has woken from her nap.

Now we stay still
For another day
Wishing and wishing
We could dance and play.

Charlie Walker (12)
Beaufort Community School, Tuffley

Heavy Sins

When the echoes of the darkness reflect,
Your senses won't be able to detect
Every single one of my den's flaws,
If you can't remember, just think of my claws.
They all had flaws, I kill 'em with claws.

He thought this was a walk in the park,
He thought it was very, very dark,
Once he saw this figure, I did bark,
Then I sliced him up, just like a shark.
They all had flaws, I kill 'em with claws.

She thought I was picking up flowers,
Oh my gawd! She had me with her powers,
Once she had me, she took me away,
After that, we both wanted to play,
They all had flaws, I kill 'em with claws.

All of these sins I have committed,
Made me think that I never fitted,
She took me, she found my surprise,
I had my pleasure, she went and cried,
They all had flaws, I kill 'em with claws.

These hands that have been soiled with blood,
Pushed me to bury my sins in mud,
The warm inside of her skin,
Turned bitter as I sliced it up so thin,
They all had flaws, I kill 'em with claws.

Long after my time,
I became a mere legend,
Because of my crimes,
They called me, 'The man of th' end'.
They all had flaws, I kill 'em with claws.

In my unmarked grave,
My head is spinning,
The only thing I now crave,
Is only a taste of sinning.

They all had flaws,
I kill 'em with claws.

Benayak Karki (12)
Beaufort Community School, Tuffley

Love

I was in love for sure,
My love for him was pure,
There was no helpful cure,
Love had to be endured,
Our love is on fire.

I've changed in every way,
Our love grows every day,
It will not fade away,
This I can safely say,
Our love is on fire.

Love will shine forever,
With the lovely weather,
We will be together,
Skin soft like a feather,
Our love is on fire.

When your smooth lips touch mine,
Our hair is like a vine,
My love for you is fine,
I can see every sign,
Our love is on fire.

Our love is very strong,
It will last very long,
Our love is on fire.

Hannah Elliss (13)
Beaufort Community School, Tuffley

The Holiday

On a day when the sun is out,
I see girls and boys scream and shout.
On the coasters the babies cry,
When it's my turn I can be shy.
When we get one thousand metres high,
I really think I'm going to die.
Even though I'm having lots of fun,
The most excited is my mum.

When in line ready for my food,
I am normally not in the mood.
And when I finally get some chips,
Surprisingly they have lots of pips.
We order our pasta,
I eat it faster.
Even though I'm having lots of fun,
The most excited is my mum.

When we arrived at our villa,
It had a humungous chiller.
In the garage it had air hockey,
And on the TV came the jockey.
In the background we had a pool,
And in the garage I played pool.
Even though I'm having lots of fun,
The most excited is my mum.

When we finally get outside,
It's shock we don't get fried.
Instead of using a great big fan,
I try my hardest to get a tan.
Even though the Earth doesn't turn,
I still capture bad sunburn.

And in America when night falls,
You are not allowed in the pool.
And when I wake up that next morning,
Throughout the day I'm still yawning.
Even though I'm having lots of fun,
The most excited is my mum.

Thomas Stevens (13)
Beaufort Community School, Tuffley

But I'm Just Going Hyper!

The moment you get a rush of excitement,
Mum says, 'Please calm down', but to have fun I shouldn't.
Jumping off tall furniture, swinging from the ceiling,
Spinning, pivoting on the spot, swirling, wheeling,
Once you start you don't know how to stop or control it,
You begin to lose your sense and start to lose your wit,
People think I'm going mad, but I'm just going hyper!

Now I'm in, there's no turning back, no stopping me now,
I'd stop if I could, but I can't, I don't know how,
You do some amusing things, stunts, when in hyper mode,
Like snow angels in vest and pants, but not feeling the cold,
It can start after eating, or just oxygen alone,
Laid screaming by the table, Mum says to lower my tone.
People think I'm going mad but I'm just going hyper!

My sister starts to laugh, but sometimes she will cry,
I don't mean to hit her hard, my bark's worse than my bite,
I go hyper at the weird time, like just before bed,
How am I to settle down, with thoughts buzzing round my head?
I try my hardest not to keep giggling, laughing or to shout,
But I will be up all night, if I don't get the hyper out,
People think I'm going mad, but I'm just going hyper!

I start to go hyper, buzzing like a bee,
I didn't know something bad would happen to me,
Had to jump over a fence, by climbing up a tree,
Foot got caught, landed on my elbow, now in A&E,
But now I'm in a cast! Back to school at last . . .
I'm in so much pain, I really hope it heals fast!
People think I'm going mad, but I'm just going hyper!

So the thing about going hyper, is it's not always good,
If I'd known what would happen, turn back the clock I would,
Some people understand, but some people just laugh,
Some people call me stupid, some call me daft,
So if you go hyper to the extreme, like I do,
Make sure what happened to me doesn't happen to you.
People thought I was going mad but I was just going hyper!

Alana Turner (13)
Beaufort Community School, Tuffley

Our Love Goes On And On!

Our feet dig in the sand,
heated by the sun. We walk
hand in hand along the beach.
Seagulls wing place to place
Our love goes on and on!

While the warm sun sets
With its stunning red,
'How radiant,' we said.
The waters are still and over the hill
Are sheep that are asleep.
Our love goes on and on!

The sun has disappeared
The mist has appeared.
We see in the distance
Our long journey home.
Our love goes on and on!

I was yours to have,
You were always mine,
We have loved each other
In and out of time.
Our love goes on and on!

When the first stone gazed
At the blazing sun
And the first tree struggled
From the forest floor
I always loved you more
Our love goes on and on!

The moon makes its way up
The stars soon follow
Our lips lock together
Wish we could stay forever
'I love you,' they chorus.
Our love goes on and on!

Stephanie Karenga (12)
Beaufort Community School, Tuffley

On the Island Of Jamaica

Lying down on that soft white beach,
Eating lime with some juicy peach,
Glad that I'm not having to teach,
On the island of Jamaica.

Standing there just ahead of me,
Is an infant boy sipping tea,
Jumping up like kids full of glee,
On the island of Jamaica.

The monkey in the tree above,
Chuckling like a tweeting dove,
I think I've just fallen in love,
On the island of Jamaica.

The climbing vines on the old wall,
Just sweetly hanging, growing tall,
This climbing vine will never fall,
On the island of Jamaica.

A shining dolphin riding by,
Makes the small children want to cry,
As it rides off under the sky,
On the island of Jamaica.

The love with me and Jamaica,
It's like a loaf and its baker,
And like mankind and its Maker,
On the island of Jamaica.

The swaying palm trees bend with ease,
Like a rose in the breeze,
Which rests over the seven seas,
On the island of Jamaica.

As the day comes close to an end,
It is your home that I must send,
All you children, this is the end,
On the island of Jamaica.

Charlotte Brain (13)
Beaufort Community School, Tuffley

War

Guns blazed and echoed around,
The traumatising, screaming sounds,
The dying and dead on the ground.
Why can't the world live in peace?

Folk are being torn apart,
Soldiers' wives have broken hearts,
They fought so hard they're in parts,
Why can't the world live in peace?

War is over stupid things,
Religion and different things,
Wives are keeping their husbands' rings,
Why can't the world live in peace?

There is not a good side,
There is not a bad side,
States hate each other 'cause they collide,
Why can't the world live in peace?

When the world has ended,
And all war wounds are mended,
The world until the very next time,
Will be at peace for a while.

Families are now distraught,
Looking at them I thought,
All the lives that have been caught,
Why can't the world live in peace?

When the war starts again,
They prepare all of their men,
Lots of dead all over again,
Why can't the world live in peace?

To the right, to the left,
They will fight till their death.
Until the end of the Earth,
Why can't the world live in peace?

Chelsea Bryon (13)
Beaufort Community School, Tuffley

A Whole Day At Beaufort School

A whole day in boring school,
I'm working like a pack mule,
All the bad kids think they're cool,
A whole day in Beaufort School.

Six lessons in just one day,
In RE we learn to pray,
And we get some holidays,
A whole day in Beaufort School.

I'm starting to like it here,
And half term is very near,
Always have to use our ears,
A whole day in Beaufort School

In science we study plants,
In geography we're on France,
At the end there'll be a dance,
A whole day in Beaufort School

English, we write a story,
It can't be a bit gory,
The teacher says she's sorry,
A whole day in Beaufort School

In maths we're doing fractions,
Gets some boring reactions,
In French we're doing actions,
A whole day in Beaufort School

In art, we paint a picture,
DT, we make a mixture,
In PE there's a fixture,
A whole day in Beaufort School

We play keyboards in music,
Homework makes me feel so sick,
In IT I enjoy it,
A whole day in Beaufort School.

Daniel Stewart (13)
Beaufort Community School, Tuffley

The Dark Deep Eyes

The dark deep eyes gazed into the night
Then they went out of sight in a quick flight
It was such a fright I held myself tight
The dark deep eyes

Their eyes blinked open as the thing yawned
As a terrifying look overtook
It was a very scary book
The dark deep eyes

He emerged from the deep dark corner
We might have been in a big dark park
I heard a big, scary, fierce dog bark
The dark deep eyes

Time seemed to travel very fast,
As things were going faster in the past
Time had finally stopped at last
The dark deep eyes

At last I was a metre away
It had been a very long unhappy day
So I went on my way, I wanted to lay
The dark deep eyes

As I was in my bed fast asleep
The dark deep eyes appeared in a beep
It made me do a very high leap
The dark deep eyes

Was it a dream or was it all real?
Was this certainly the real deal?
I woke up in pain and agony
The dark deep eyes

That very night was the last breath I took
It must have been the dark green look that overtook
The dark deep eyes.

Emma Philip (12)
Beaufort Community School, Tuffley

The Match

This could be the best match ever
Cricket could have never been at its best
You wouldn't see a match like this, never
And the coin toss made it a test

The home team was known as the 'Great'
The away team are known as the 'Worst'
The home team was expecting a win but they would have to wait
As one player for the 'Worst' was ready to burst.

As Tendulkar and Selwag walked out the ground
The bowling attack of Anderson and Hutchinson
Was ready to attack as the ball was going to take a pound
But the 'Worst' knew this was gonna be fun.

Tendulkar and Selwag were hitting every ball
They kept on scoring sixes and fours
And the defence of these two was like a door
Then this ball was bowled to Tendulkar and he was no more

The ball was bowled, the batsman missed it
Another ball, the batsman missed it
He knew he had to hit to score and he had hit
The last ball bowled, the batsman swung for it like a twit.

After all the boredom of cricket,
The final ball arrived with the home team on 279 - 7
Then Hutchinson ran up and bowled a ball so fast
for someone so small.
So they were all over, they felt it was a job well done.

As Hutchinson came out with Bob
Needing 280 to win, the 'worst' was ready
The best came steaming in with a new job
To get players out with a brand new ball, they were steady

As wickets fell Hutchinson and Anderson
Were left with a ball and their target was done.

Jordan Hutchinson (12)
Beaufort Community School, Tuffley

Man Vs Nature

A waving tree
on islands be
the sand gleams
as children scream.

Guns blazing
shell casings
on a beach
as children scream.

Bodies are down
planes have crashed
I had to frown
as children scream.

Houses burnt to the ground
charred bodies all around
no end is in sight
it could take about four years
still children scream.

Three years later
people face her
the queen of queens
nature strikes again
children scream.

The blood and gore
on civilians' doors
the children scream
how they do scream.

The blood that pours
face her claws
all is quiet
all is calm
children scream no more.

Joshua Dowd (13)
Beaufort Community School, Tuffley

Life

Life is weird and wonderful
But it's always quite strange
You always hear complaints and cheer
Things that you regularly hear
But in the end you're fine again

Life has many ups and down
In many different people's minds
Life is extremely hard
Which makes people very stressed
But whatever you do it's wrong

Life is full of different things
Fairy tales are not what you see
Everybody has their days
Even if they are quite strange
But in the end you're fine again

Life is seen in many ways
By people in the little days
Life depends on people's ways
Even if they are quite strange
Life is cool in many ways

Life is full of many names
In many different moods and days
Everybody is not the same
Especially when they are strange
As life comes to an end.

It is starting to slow down
As then you start to realise
Life is always around
But in the end it is quite great
Don't let go until you know
Your life has been very great.

Shannon Kelly (13)
Beaufort Community School, Tuffley

Die For Love

As she looks into the mirror,
she sees herself quivering with fear,
her bloodshot eyes burning up in anger,
how could someone have done this to her?
What has she done?

She clenches her fists,
and scratches her wrists.
'Why me?' she whispers
her life disappears.
What has she done?

She stares into her own dull eyes,
they hold her emotions through surprise,
she stares down to the ground
and her empty hearty starts to pound.
What has she done?

And she drops to the ground,
and she doesn't even make a sound.
As the last tear falls,
the engine of a motorbike roars.
What has she done?

A life that day, was lost for love,
as special as a crystal-white dove.
She took too many pills knowing her fate,
but the paramedics were too late.
What did she do?

And she was put to rest,
looking at her very best,
her hand on her cold heart
and the young dark boy whispers,
'Til death do us part.'

Courtney Wood (12)
Beaufort Community School, Tuffley

Hated!

She was smothered in hate,
Wished it could change but it was too late,
She didn't know where she stood,
She would have them back if she could,
She was all alone.

Alone in the dark,
It broke her heart,
She needed to cry,
She wished she could die,
She was all alone.

Walking in pain,
She was going insane,
It was never shown,
But she was on her own,
She was all alone.

She wanted to hold her head high,
But all she could do was cry,
She was stood in the rain,
It was hard to see her pain,
She was all alone.

She just wanted to go,
But her parents were telling her no,
She just needed that one friend,
It was driving her around the bend,
She was all alone.

Constant hurt inside,
She had no pride,
She hated feeling this way,
But she had nothing else to say,
She was all alone.

Courtney Hodges (13)
Beaufort Community School, Tuffley

A Shinigami Death Note

I found a book left on the floor
I picked it up and locked the door
To my dismay I gazed in awe
A god of death came through my wall
A Shinigami death note

In the book there were lots of rules
I read the book and read and read
I wrote a name and found him dead
The person died because of me
A Shinigami death note

I turned the television on
I knew that there was something wrong
I saw a person kill someone
I wrote them down and down they fell
A Shinigami death note

I watched the late night news in fear
I knew that someone would be near
My sister dropped her lemon curd
She didn't believe what she heard
A Shinigami death note

The police are now on my case
I am going to make them chase
I am sure I will win this race
So I'll have to keep up the pace
A Shinigami death note

Got cornered by a guy called L
'I'll kill you,' he began to yell
'I will send you right into Hell!'
I know that this will not go well
A Shinigami death note.

Kayleigh Andrews (12)
Beaufort Community School, Tuffley

In Your Dreams

In your dreams, the clouds are fluffy
They are all so pink and puffy
As they are all floating past
It seems as if life goes so fast
In your dreams

In your dreams, the rainbow shines
All the pretty colours in lines
As you watch them up above
You may even see a crystal dove
In your dreams

In your dreams, the flowers bloom
As you lie there in your room
Whilst you watch them all sprout out
And you may hear a tiny shout
In your dreams

In your dreams the waterfalls fall
Underneath the big town hall
The sound of water hits you
It will make you need the loo
In your dreams

In your dreams the sun shines high
Right up in that lush blue sky
If you look up at the night
It will never look so bright
In your dreams

In your dreams you will sleep
In your bed counting sheep
As one takes a big leap
You may wake from your sleep
In your dreams.

Sian Scarratt (13)
Beaufort Community School, Tuffley

The Meadow

Birdsong fills the air with cheer,
Ringing through the valley clear.
When the end of day is near,
The moonlight shines like a tear.
When the meadow comes alive.

At day the flowers grow and bloom,
The tall, towering trees loom.
New life awaiting in cocoons,
Foxes howling at the moon.
When the meadow comes alive.

Huge fields of verdant green grass,
The memories here won't pass.
The good times will always last,
Let's not look back at the past.
When the meadow comes alive.

Butterflies dance in the air,
Swirling round without a care.
Rabbits bouncing in pairs,
The love here will never tear.
When the meadow comes alive.

The beautiful sapphire skies,
Under it everyone lies.
Huge plains of barley and rye,
Wonderful views, maybe you sigh.
When the meadow comes alive

When the sun must go away,
Everyone must finish play.
This must happen every day,
The sky will never turn grey.
When the meadow comes alive.

Georgia Sandford (13)
Beaufort Community School, Tuffley

Love Wasn't For Him

He was grand, he was sweet.
She was horrible, she was meat.
He wanted her so.
But she wanted to go.
Love wasn't for him.

She wasn't right.
But he had to fight.
She left him there.
Without a care.
Love wasn't for him.

He wanted to cry.
But she had to lie.
She felt alright.
But he still wanted to fight.
Love wasn't for him.

She walked away.
But he had to stay.
She loved him so.
But she never did show.
Love wasn't for him.

He was at home.
She was alone.
He thought of her night and day.
All he could do was pray.
Love wasn't for him.

He couldn't take it anymore.
He had to go.
He got a gun
And shot himself to the floor.
Love wasn't for him.

Leah Robinson (13)
Beaufort Community School, Tuffley

My Cousin Rhys

Meet my family's new addition
So handsome, sweet and smart
With a look, he'll have you smiling
With a chuckle he'll own your heart
My cousin Rhys!

His skin so soft, he smells so nice
Hair so wild, with bouncing curls
Teeth just peeking through
Like little tiny pearls
My cousin Rhys!

His favourite show is 'Chuggington'!
He claps and cheers along
Watching all the trains go by
He loves to hear the song
My cousin Rhys!

Trips to the park
Playing on the swings
'Seesaw, seesaw!'
He loves to hear us sing!
My cousin Rhys!

To settle down he must have Doug
And with a hug from Mum
Slowly drifting off to sleep
Whilst sucking on his thumb
My cousin Rhys!

He's growing up so very quickly
These days go by so fast
Hold him tight and love him dearly
Make these precious moments last
My cousin Rhys!

Amy Balding (13)
Beaufort Community School, Tuffley

Mysterious Creature Of The Sea

Plumes of bubbles swarm the sea,
Plankton dance through the waves with glee
But then the creature of the sea,
Appears so very suddenly.

His petrol fins house his power,
He slides and glides hour by hour
He is as gentle as can be,
He is the creature of the sea.

His sparkling, blue, slimy blubber,
Keeps him from the freezing weather
Wide bright eyes can spot his prey,
A bloom of seaweed or plankton he'll swallow today.

His huge weight and capacity,
Frighten all of those below the sea
But he doesn't feast on huge fish or any meat,
Plants and plankton are his only treat.

His petrol fins house his power,
He slides and glides hour by hour
He is as calm as the waves,
He flaps his fins all of the day.

He wanders alone through the sea,
Trying to find his family
But they have all been poached and taken away,
That's why we have to help them today.

All of the creatures in the sea have to be kept in harmony,
Let's love and care for the world today
To spare the lives of innocent animals
Like the creature of the sea!

Whale!

Megan Reeves (12)
Beaufort Community School, Tuffley

The Passion Of Love!

People express that love hurts,
But rejection destroys you,
Love is a beautiful thing,
If you find that special someone,
Passion is undesirable,
But ending it hurts the most.

Dreaming about them all day long,
Being together is like heaven,
But it can tear you apart,
Thinking about them all day,
It's such a beautiful thing,
But ending it hurts the most,

They make you feel so special,
They always make sure you're careful,
Looking up at the blazing stars,
And seeing their appearance,
Without any interference,
But ending it hurts the most,

Sitting under the stars at night,
Holding each other so close,
Loving every moment of it,
Oh how do I adore you?
Your fragrance lifts me off my feet,
But ending it hurts the most,

I looked up into his eyes,
And the butterflies burst out,
Oh how much do I love you?
Always having a good time,
The feeling is amazing,
But ending it hurts the most.

Taylor Sandford (13)
Beaufort Community School, Tuffley

Sam And Dayna

Hot sun beaming down on the ground,
Romance is here and all around
Sam and Dayna were on the sand,
walking together hand in hand.
They loved each other,
and were together forever.

'I love you,' Dayna replied,
whilst Sam gazed into her eyes.
The wind blew Dayna's brown hair,
whilst small, shy Sam stopped and stared.
They loved each other,
and were together forever.

The aqua sea ate the sand,
as it headed towards the land.
The fish swam rapidly around
whilst tiny Sam looked at the clouds.
They loved each other,
and were together forever.

As they sat on the golden sand
still holding each other's hands,
Sam kissed her rosy-red cheek
as the seagulls squawked and squeaked.
They loved each other,
and were together forever.

Their heads were close together
their lips redder than ever.
They slowly kissed each other
whilst being alone together.
They loved each other,
and were happy forever.

Jessica Crane (13)
Beaufort Community School, Tuffley

Something Wasn't Right

She was as bright as the stars above them
He was so deeply, utterly in love
They first met underneath the moonlight.
Above all that they loved each other
But her mother disapproved of him.
She thought that they would last forever
He thought that he might end it that night.
They were in love, but something wasn't right.

He left her at that, thereon she sat,
Dreaming that they could have had a future
Her mother wanted the best for her
But hated the sight of this upset,
She tried talking to her troubled daughter
But worryingly got no true answer.
She had never seen her daughter like this.
She loved her daughter, but something wasn't right.

Then he realised he needed her
So he travelled far just to see her
He begged on his knees for her forgiveness
Her brain told her a definite no!
But she listened to her heart saying, 'Go!'
They shared their love like the stars above
Something so special was there that night
They loved each other and then it felt right.

Her mum accepted the man she married
They were as happy as could be
He never left her again after that
She loved him more than anything else
They are now a happy family
They love each other and now it feels right.

Chelsea Burnham (12)
Beaufort Community School, Tuffley

My Journey Home

I walk outside on a hot summer's day
head held high as I walk on by,
see the birds sit and look at me pleased
as the sun shines in the sky so high,
gardens full of flowers and weeds

I smell the flowers as I walk along,
teasing the wasps and the bees,
feels like nothing can go wrong,
I feel the grass on my knees,
the river playing a secret song

I listen to the stream trickle on by,
wave to all on my journey down,
I slowly do up my Beaufort tie,
as my feet walk along the ground,
I gaze up at the blue sky

I see the children playing games,
kicking, laughing, enjoying themselves
and the wind is tamed
I walk to the shop and search the shelves
I reach for the Coke within

I listen to the stream trickle on by
wave to all on my journey down
I slowly do up my tie
as my feet walk along the ground
I gaze at the blue sky

I smell the flowers as I walk along
teasing the wasps and bees.
it feels like nothing can go wrong,
grass on my knees, the river playing a secret song.

Lauren Louise Stroud (13)
Beaufort Community School, Tuffley

Unfortunate Love

The blossom fell onto the fresh grass
As the young girl cried into her hands
About how she lost her love
Oh the sweet cries of a young girl
For only her love to hear

Just to know that he wouldn't hear
Upset the young girl with tears
She imagined love
As the feel of the finest silk
The biggest thrill in life
The sound of happiness
And the look of the colour red

Suddenly the wind hushed
It was a deafening silence
The gates opened with a rush
On that rough, dreary night,
She cried and cried herself to sleep
Hoping for her love to know
The soft cries of a young girl.

A letter appeared
A soft, fresh, white letter
She opened it with shaky hands
Hoping hard it was from her love
But sadly it wasn't.

That day she realised
That her one and only love
Would never be seen.

Laura Beacham (12)
Beaufort Community School, Tuffley

The Magic Of The World Cup

Spain, I want them to win.
Torres, as sharp as a pin.

Portugal, our neighbours.
Ronaldo, diving again

Beckham injured and out.
Terry no longer captain.

South Africa, the hosts.
However not the favourites.

Italy, title holders.
The players, getting older.

Henry, the star up front
Ribery, the cool winger.

Germany, the last to host.
Can South Africa top it?

Brazil, skilful and strong.
Robinho's dazzling feet.

Netherlands, yoyo team.
van Persie, in terrific form.

Ivory Coast, small place.
Drogba, strong and powerful.

Only the best can win.
The fans, roaring themselves hoarse.
Stunning skill and quick feet.
World Cup, magical contest!

Steven Bevan (12)
Beaufort Community School, Tuffley

In Your Dreams

Birds chirping in the sky,
As the cold wind blows by,
Not a grey cloud in sight,
With the sun very bright,
In your dreams.

Butterflies in the air,
With grass as fine as hair,
Teeny lambs are just born,
Wait a bit for the horns,
In your dreams.

A fast-flowing river,
You feel a small shiver,
Someone catches your eye,
As he goes swimming by,
In your dreams.

'Come out and talk to me,
Please, please, don't leave me be,
I think you're really fit,
And I love you to bits,'
She sang in her dream.

The current came quickly,
The rocks were quite prickly,
Then she heard a smash,
And her lover crashed,
And that was the end of her dream.

Hannah Jones (13)
Beaufort Community School, Tuffley

Beware Of The Tigers!

Predators, beasts,
Mammals and hunters,
Parents and newborns,
Beware! For these are the tigers.

Daniela Valkova (11)
Beaufort Community School, Tuffley

The Dreaded Supply

The day has come
The day that's hated
It's a supply
She's extremely low-rated

        We need a way
        To get rid of her
        The whole class is terrified
        We need back Sir

I'll get on the blower
And phone up Captain Cook
He'll understand our desperate needs
And he'll give her the hook

        I'll recruit the British tanks
        To go and run her down
        There will be no more Miss Supply
        She'll be flattened to the ground

I'll build a massive catapult
And tell her to sit in her chair
She'll be fired miles away
Come back, she wouldn't dare!

I hope there's never a day like this!
It's the complete opposite to bliss!

Owen Jones (11)
Beaufort Community School, Tuffley

Soldiers Of The Wastelands

Bodies all around me,
No one is full of glee,
Bullets are flying,
Return of their firing.

We are the soldiers that defend your lands,
The blood of others is upon our hands.

My ears are blown
Feeling all alone,
Missing my family,
A bullet wound on my knee.

We are the soldiers that defend your lands,
The blood of others is upon our hands.

The explosion of bombs,
Faint voices coming over the comms,
Blood and dirt on my face,
I have bigger worries than an undone shoelace.

We are the soldiers that defend your lands,
The blood of others is upon our hands.

Timothy Reeves (12)
Beaufort Community School, Tuffley

Snow Fun

Children running and playing in the snow.
Making snowmen and throwing snowballs,
ducking and diving behind small snow walls.

Sledging down the hill.
Whizzing past and crashing into a tree,
going so fast, bruising the knee.

After a day in the snow, it's time to go home.
Squelching inside, soaked to the bone,
the newly made snowman standing all alone.

John Pemberton (11)
Beaufort Community School, Tuffley

The Silky Sea And Beautiful Beaches

Far in the distance,
Where the sun is out,
There's a quiet place,
That we dream about,

The sea is gentle and relaxed,
The beach is quiet and never packed,
Hear the soft waves wash onto the shore,
The sun's so hot you can barely touch the floor,

The sea is turquoise,
It shines like diamonds in the sun,
You feel like you're in a microwave,
Cooking like a bun,

Then the waves turn slow,
The sun goes down,
And silence passes through the town,

The beach falls to sleep,
Till morning comes,
Then waiting for the rising sun.

Jordan Lord (12)
Beaufort Community School, Tuffley

Snooker

I come to the table with my cue,
I pot a red,
I pot a blue.

This is what I do
It is really fun
You could do it too.

I need one more ball
It is really hard
Because I am only small.

Ryan Shepherd (12)
Beaufort Community School, Tuffley

David Cameron Laughs

Look at Gordon Brown,
He doesn't even smile,
He only knows how to frown,
Although he does once in a while.

You must've seen it on TV,
So go and put on your coat,
Not the adverts 'Love, Love TV',
The one where you go and vote.

If I were to win,
All the rest would be in a sin bin,
Doing all that work,
It would make me thin!

So please put on your coat,
Before you do, put on a shoe,
Then come and vote,
It would change everything I do.

Craig Pierce (12)
Beaufort Community School, Tuffley

Dungeons

The tickets rest like a rock,
In the warm, clammy hand,
People stood gazing in a flock.

Moving up in the queue,
Mysterious noises coming from deep within,
Waiting for their chance.

The dungeons are waiting . . .
Waiting for customers
For them to start hating!

Shivering with cold but also fear,
Nearly inside but feeling the excitement,
Hearing the piercing screeching!

Charlotte Bailes (12)
Beaufort Community School, Tuffley

Parkour

You gotta be strong
you gotta be quick
you gotta be skilful
not scared of the trick

this is parkour
this is free running
this is style
the reactions are stunning

you gotta show the world
you gotta feel free
you gotta loosen up
to vault like me

this is my life
this is my hobby
it starts the adrenaline
that feeds my body.

Dan Langley (12)
Beaufort Community School, Tuffley

Sunny Summer Holidays

People relax
And sunbathe by the sea
The sun in the sky
Shines down happily

The pool filled with people
As they play beach ball
The seats are all taken
In the dining hall

Summer is great
Summer is fun
Now let's go and play
Under the sun.

Harriet Fortey (12)
Beaufort Community School, Tuffley

Kitten To A Cat

My mum gives birth to me,
Small, cute and furry,
My eyes open slowly,
And I am not lonely.

All from the same mister,
I am the sixth sister,
With my only brother,
Who's so special to my mother.

We all gather round to have a feed,
We all take turns, that's what we've agreed,
As Mother's milk helps us grow,
Drinking it all very slow.

As I grow older I lie around,
Relaxing without a sound,
I cuddle up to my sisters and brother,
Unfortunately without my mother.

Rhiannon Eveleigh (12)
Beaufort Community School, Tuffley

Full Moon

All day he is human
Like everyone else
But when full moon is here
The beast lurks about

He visits little children
Feasts upon their flesh
Parents wake to horror
To see their children dead

Whenever it's full moon
Parents lock away
As it's never safe, when
Werewolves feed again.

Kieran McDonagh (12)
Beaufort Community School, Tuffley

Newborn Puppies

Puppies crawl on the floor,
Just born from their mum,
Brothers, sisters at the door,
To see the morning sun.

> They eat with their tiny tongues,
> Tiny paws struggle to stand,
> In the morning a little bird sang,
> Puppies in their owner's hand.

Their small blue eyes stare,
Their owner walks the mother,
As I stand there looking scared,
With all my sisters and brothers.

> My brother is very small,
> My sister is quite shy,
> My mother's fairly tall,
> My father is very sly.

Michelle Hodge (12)
Beaufort Community School, Tuffley

Summer Scenes

The beach is glowing
Bright sun is shining
And kids are by the sea

Scorching sun rising
Bright clean water glimmers
And waves crash fiercely

The adults surfing
Children make sandcastles
And enjoy the summer scenes.

Rebecca Lawrence (11)
Beaufort Community School, Tuffley

Death

The Earth is slowly dying.
Exhausts bursting out pollution into the air.
The drivers in the cars,
Just don't care.

The ice is melting,
The sea is rising,
The land is decreasing
And the ocean is increasing.

The trees are falling,
Day by day.
The animals are suffering,
Week by week.

Innocent people dying every day,
They've got no food, no money,
Nothing at all.
Whose fault is it?

Rebecca Riselli (12)
Beaufort Community School, Tuffley

Boom, Boom, Clap!

Boom, boom, clap!
Goes the drum,
On my guitar I strum,
A beat comes along,
That goes with my song.

Boom, boom, clap!
On my lap,
There's no time for naps,
Come on and clap,
And listen to my rap.

Boom, boom, clap!
Now the piano comes in,
My song will be over in a min',
At the end, I start to snap,
If you enjoyed it,
You will clap.

Amreet Kaur Atwal (12)
Beaufort Community School, Tuffley

Falaq . . .

Falaq is a turquoise dress that sparkles every move.
She is a breathtaking dress that gives an elegant flow on each step.
She is a showpiece, the centre of attention.
She is a grand dancing dress that twirls with swirls.

Falaq is an exotic, flourishing rose that leaves her rich scent everywhere.
A unique flower that brightens up the day.
She is a blossoming rose, so small yet explosive with her colours.
She attracts the insects with her fragrance and luminous colour.

My sister is the colour sky-blue.
Falaq is the finest kind of blue.
She is calm and very open.
She releases the clouds and reflects the sunlight onto Earth.
She is a bright, straightforward and approachable blue.

Falaq is the sea; this sea is deep and emotional.
You could gaze at her for days and not get tired.
She is a reserved sea, so stunning and clear.
This sea has diving mermaids and somersaulting dolphins, almost like a fairy tale.

Falaq is the sound of laughter, she would laugh
as if she had never laughed before.
Her laugh would make the world smile with her glow.
She is the delightful sound of laughter because her laugh
is bursting and never stops.

Falaq is the sunny weather.
She is the sun that shines brightly across the horizon.
This sun shoots its rays over the wild, sizzling, sandy beach full of nature.
She overpowers the blue sky with her beam.
You could not live without her warm weather,

Tasmia Asif (12)
Challney High School for Girls, Luton

My Mother

She is as happy as the sun shining bright,
High up in the fluffy clouds,
Resting quietly in peace,
Up bright and early in the morning.

She is a beautiful aeroplane flying over a rainbow,
Gliding and swaying in the trees and bushes,
Flying over the Eiffel Tower,
Looking at all the world down below.

She is a garden full of bright, blossomed flowers,
With all the colours of the rainbow,
Getting showered in the refreshing water,
And slowly getting pushed side to side in the light wind.

She is a delicate pink flower in her garden,
A flower that is never lonely,
A flower that always has someone to talk to,
A flower that never gets bored listening to others.

She is a fascinating blue and pink sky on a 6pm evening,
A wonderful sight to look at every day,
Because she is always as bright as a rainbow,
And always as happy as a bunny.

She is as sweet as strawberry milkshake,
Soft, fluffy and bubbly,
As calm as the strawberries inside,
In a fancy glass sitting on the window ledge.

She is a big, red, juicy strawberry,
Filled with love and happiness,
A strawberry that has no enemy,
A special strawberry loved by me . . .
                        My mother . . .

Kainaat Sheikh (12)
Challney High School for Girls, Luton

Message To The BNP

BNP want to turn this into a 'white land',
But I'm going to win this fight and get everybody's hands in the air,
Say goodbye to the fascism and the racism,
Because there are little kids living in war zones hiding behind cones,
Praying to God they don't get shot,
Pick up their little brother from the cot,
He's crying,
Because in front of his hidden eyes, Mum's dying,
Lying in a pool of blood,
No idea where their dad's at,
He might be beaten by a bat,
All that goes on in their minds
Is that they've got to get out of this country before they go blind.
At the age of twelve he has to raise a family of four,
What more
Do you want?
So Nick Griffin
I hope you're listening
Because this poem isn't dissing,
Don't be missing the point,
All I'm trying to say is it doesn't matter if you're black,
Brown or white,
We bleed the same colour blood,
So I'm going to represent the people,
Those that are hurting,
While I'm splurting my verses,
I'm going to try and lift all the curses.

Almira Rafeeque (15)
Challney High School for Girls, Luton

Ibraheem

He is a green T-shirt with splashes of paint,
leaving an insight of happiness dazzling others.

He is a roaring plane, loud and explosive,
frantically chasing his mother.

He is a wildflower, small but strong
blossoming all year round.

He is cold Coca-cola, bubbly and fizzy,
a burst of energy waiting to be found.

He is the daytime, when the sun is alive,
with an eager face that makes my day.

He is a vibrant yellow, bright and joyful,
forever ready to play.

He is a savannah, with space to run free.
He is the grass stretching everywhere.

He is a firework, spontaneous and dazzling,
lighting up the sky as much as it dares.

He is the powerful trumpet being blown,
a light laughter spreading all around.

He is the first snow of winter, gracefully sweeping the nation,
his smile lighting up this whole town.

Sabeera Dar (13)
Challney High School for Girls, Luton

Mum . . .

She is a colourful blue T-shirt full
of designs with lots of bright sequins.

She is a fast working Ferrari, full
of energy and excitement, she is never tired.

She grows gracefully, like a rose.
She is peaceful and beautiful.

She would be a very tasty, nice, warm,
hot chocolate with cream, marshmallows
and sprinkles of chocolate.

She is a 7.30am person who is ready to start
a fresh day and have a great day.

The colour, I think she is blue because
she is a peaceful, nice and calm person.

She is from a place like Dubai, always calm and happy.
She is soft as sand.

She is a sound of laughter when people are
talking in a group,

She is a fine summer's day, with a cool breeze,
because she is calm and cool when she is angry.

Tasnima Ahmed (13)
Challney High School for Girls, Luton

Cottage So Spooky

She wandered lonely through the wood,
terrified and alone, there she stood.
She saw a spooky cottage nearby,
webbed, dirty, dusty, there it did lie.

'Enter,' said a deep scary voice,
her hand upon the door, what was her choice?
She opened the door and took one step in,
the only thing she saw was a light very dim.

Shadows cast and her heart was pounding.
'Come in,' said the same voice but more terrifying.
She took a few more steps in, taking care,
as she did, she saw a rocking chair.

With a blink of an eye, a horrifying man appeared,
blood tricking down his head, was what she had feared.
he drew out an axe and came so close.
She shouted, 'What do you want from me?'
He replied, 'Soul, soul, soul!'

He roared a horrifying roar
and slit her throat,
that was it, the end, there was no more.

Kiran Riaz (13)
Challney High School for Girls, Luton

The Hidden Door

She wandered lonely through the woods.
Terrified and lonely there she stood.
Terrified as something pulled her hood.
As she turned she thought of her neighbourhood.

When she knocked on the crooked door,
She felt something open in the path floor.
There she stood, waiting and watching.
It was another small door.

When she saw it clearly appear,
She never thought it could disappear.
As she froze it came more near,
She was about to explode with that amount of fear.

The door opened and whispered, 'Hello.'
When she bent over she saw something yellow.
Gleaming and sparkling it kept whispering, 'Hello.'
There it was, her grandma's gold necklace.

She looked around to find help.
It sucked her in as she yelped.
She felt a bony hand pull her up,
As if it was crushing a delicate china cup . . .

Muneebah Bashrat (13)
Challney High School for Girls, Luton

My Little Sister . . .

She is an adventurous aeroplane,
Soaring over colourful rainbows.

She is a glass of refreshing lemonade,
all tangy and icy, perfect for a hot summer's day.

She is a pretty little summer dress,
With bright colourful flowers blooming out.

She is a sweet, juicy strawberry,
Filled with joy and excitement.

She is the rich colour of purple,
When the sun sets over the horizon.

She is a big, beautiful garden,
Blooming with every colour of the rainbow.

She is the innocent pink blossom flowers of spring,
And the graceful golden leaves of autumn.

She is the relaxing warmth of the sunshine,
Beaming over playful children.

She is the first little giggle of laughter,
Coming from a sweet little baby.

Amina Rizvi (13)
Challney High School for Girls, Luton

My Sister Sameen

She is a flowing yellow dress,
With bright red sparks of polka dots sprinkled everywhere.

She is a fiery, fast-paced motorbike,
Screeching and loud as ever.

She is a sensitive, gentle daisy,
Blossoming upwards and out.

She is cool, fizzing cherryade in a glass,
Bubbles frothing out over the top.

She is the time of day when the sun is rising,
Sometimes soothing, sometimes frustrating.

She is the most precious, priceless gold,
The dazzling treasure chest marked spot - X.

She is a glowing, helium balloon,
Big explosions and bangs here and there.

She is the warm, bright smile of the sunshine,
As happy and shining as can be!

Sehar Ahmad (12)
Challney High School for Girls, Luton

. . . She Is The Darkness And The Light . . .

She is a designer, silky dress with bright sequins and dark colours of swirls, shimmering in the blackness of the dress.

She is a sparkling silver Aston Martin standing out in the sunlight, advancing briskly on the clean road with a powerful engine.

She is a long, skinny stem with an exotic, smooth, beautiful flower with smooth, sharp petals which are dark, silky violet.

She is an icy, refreshing, heavenly tropical drink with the taste of paradise served in a shiny, neatly curved high-quality glass.

She is dark, silent midnight with swirls of darkness and strips of light above lit up, basking in the shine of the moonlight.

She is a varied range of exciting bright colour, which is a large explosion of fireworks and rainbows in the night.

She is a loud, but graceful, huge bang of medium pitch tweeting, but also vigorously and hardcore constantly till the end.

She is the bright, reflecting sun in the baby-blue sky with a mist of fluffy clouds sailing past onboard the powerful galleon.

Simranpreet Kaur Summan (12)
Challney High School for Girls, Luton

She Is A . . .

She is a hot pink T-shirt with black splatters.
Dark and wise, yet sweet and sensitive.

A motorcycle with the ultimate sound and speed.
She's fast and will always catch up.

A soft rose with smooth pure petals.
She puts a smile on anybody's face.

She is a dance club full of hype.
Life of the party, never frowns.

A guitar with a heavy bass.
Sounds amazing all the time.

A midday person, she loves to go out.
Meeting her friends, shopping and always hyper.

She's a can of Coke, bubbly and fizzy.
If you shake it, it will explode.

Summer describes her well, as it's her favourite season.
But don't get too close or you'll get burnt.

Afeera Jamil (13)
Challney High School for Girls, Luton

A Special Person

She is a pretty pink dress in the morning sun, gleaming and
glistening, made of silk.
She's a plane flying high in the sky, diving up and down,
swooping and swerving, making a soft trail.
She's a red rose in the summer at full bloom with peace in the
surroundings, soft and spherical.
She's a glass of swirly hot chocolate drink with sprinkles on top,
a warm mouth-watering feeling.
She's the light of dawn when the sky is a rainbow coming up
onto the world.
She's a twinkly baby-blue with a hint of hot pink in the middle.
She's the Tower Bridge at night, lit up and shining bright,
so kind to let all the cars and ships through.
She's a silent tone with a soothing feeling, giving me peace
and happiness going deep into my heart.
She's a sunny summer's day when everyone's on the beach
shimmering onto the ocean, reflecting from place to place.
She's the best! My cousin Husna . . .

Amna Tariq (13)
Challney High School for Girls, Luton

House 16

House 16. The biggest house on Flower Close Road.
Owned and lived in by some old guy and his family,
All killed by assassins.

Now haunted by the ghosts of the living dead.
People went in, never came out.

Should I go in? What will I find?
I reach out for the handle,
But then the door turns into a dream
Showing the night of the murders.
I see it all.

Then it all goes black.

Euan Jephcote (12)
Churchdown School, Churchdown

My Dear Elephant

Elephant, Elephant,
What can I do?
My heart and sorrow
I send to you.

A shot of a gun,
One bang, and you're gone,
Ornaments for a fine place,
Tusks for a piano.

Elephant, Elephant,
You're my best friend,
Why do they do this?
Is it easy to mend?

Elephant . . .

A shot of a gun,
One bang, and you're gone,
Ornaments for a fine place,
Tusks for a piano.

Elephant, Elephant,
My Lord I pray,
Stop, stop this!
Do you hear me say?

Elephant . . .

A shot of a gun,
One bang, and you're gone,
Ornaments for a fine place,
Tusks for a piano.

Elephant, Elephant,
It's illegal now,
You're safe with me
No longer will you bow.

Elephant . . .

No shot of a gun,
And no bang, you're not gone,
No ornament for a fireplace
No tusks for a piano!

Emily Garfield (13)
Churchdown School, Churchdown

The House!

Nobody ever went in, nobody ever went out . . .

I'm standing by it, suddenly I hear a shout.
What could it be, I wonder?
Or even who could it be?
I'm shivering, really scared,
Not knowing whether to go in or just walk away.
After a moment of thinking I decide to stay.

Slowly I open the door.
I creep in.
'Argh!' I scream
Someone's looking right my way.
They keep following me everywhere.

I'm horrified now. The door won't open, I'm stuck.
There's nowhere to go.
Am I going to get shot?
Will I ever get out alive?
'Ho, ho, ho, you'll never know!' I hear someone say.
The gun's aimed at my head.
All I want to be doing now is be tucked up in my bed.

Boom! Bang!
Bullets are fired at me.
I scream
Then wake up.

Oh, it was just a dream!

Edie Stone (12)
Churchdown School, Churchdown

The Stairs

You
 walk
  down
   the
    stairs
     and
      they
       creak
        like
         coals
          in
           a
            fire

They
 seem
  to
   go
    on
     for
      ever
       . . .
        An
         eternal
          walk

Your
 legs
  begin
   to
    tire
     as
      you
       walk
        down
         down
          down . . .

            down the stairs.

Nathan Evans (13)
Churchdown School, Churchdown

Dead

Dark, damp, cold, gloomy
I live in a tower
by the clock
that strikes the hour

People passing
every day
telling the time
while on their way

In a cold wind
the sound I heard
under its breath
not a single word

I clutched a thorn
I began to scream
the light turned on
it was just a dream

A child looked up
this one day
I was so happy
I wanted to stay

I could not speak
I could not stay
It wasn't safe here
I was too late and there I lay.

Sam Pennington (13)
Churchdown School, Churchdown

Depressing Wedding

I hoped I would stay wed,
Until I was dead.
This may be sad
But I promise I'm not mad.

When I slipped into my white dress,
I felt like a million dollars.
Hair up, make-up done nice.
I opened the doors and started walking.

I hoped I would stay wed,
Until I was dead.
This may be sad
But I promise I'm not mad.

When I looked into my husband-to-be's eyes,
I felt like I was in Heaven.
And suddenly I realised that was where I wanted to be.
Either that or Hell!

I hoped I would stay wed,
Until I was dead.
This may be sad
But I promise I'm not mad.

The wedding depressed me.
But I have gone now.

Amy-Jo Taylor (12)
Churchdown School, Churchdown

Mrs Troubles And Her Bubbles

Mrs Troubles like playing with bubbles,
Bubbles was her favourite thing to stop all of her troubles,
When she had troubles, she got out her bottle of bubbles,
Eventually she stopped all of her trouble
So she could chuck out her bottle of bubbles
and have no troubles!

Lauren Knight (12)
Churchdown School, Churchdown

It's Locked!

Sat in a corner,
damp and cold,
dust and dirty,
grey and old.

>Clinking padlock,
>see the chain,
>wondering if it'll ever
>open again.

>>Eyes cutting through,
>>the darkness holds me tight,
>>escape plan, I think,
>>I may be bright.

>>>This isn't easy,
>>>I'm feeling queasy,
>>>lack of food,
>>>it's locked.

The padlock, hard as stone,
no one knows I'm here,
I'm just skin and bone,
I can't break free.

>It's locked.

Bethan Heather Richards (13)
Churchdown School, Churchdown

Football Star

He is the best striker in the world.
All of his shots will go in.
Goalies shake with fear as he comes with the ball.
Defenders can't do a thing.
Midfielders just aren't fast enough.
Goal after goal.
Too bad he isn't real!

Jake Wolstencroft (12)
Churchdown School, Churchdown

Zero Hour

The clock is ticking,
Ticking down.
Men are smoking all around,
Boys are crying, they are just too young.

It was not their choice,
Not at all.
They had to go, they were told,
But they did not know where they were.

The clock is ticking,
Ticking down.
Men are smoking all around,
Boys are crying, they are just too young.

Bullets whistling overhead,
'Thirty seconds,' the driver said.
All the men and boys going in,
Half will die, half will live.

The ramp has dropped, they must go.
They just have to run and pray.
'Lord, what will happen to me?'
They all ask, for it is now
Zero hour!

Ryan Harris (12)
Churchdown School, Churchdown

The Arc

You walk slowly through the corridors of the arc,
Silence is upon you until you reach the dark.
The arc will always be here, don't be afraid,
The days of justice will soon now be made.
Some deaths that the arc has been gladly given,
But some will never ever, ever, ever be forgiven.
The arc is small but has infinite black room,
The blackness kills whatever enters the creepy, haunted gloom.

Macauley Medcroft (13)
Churchdown School, Churchdown

Street Life

Life on the street has no bonus.
Every day I long to have a home.
Every day I long to be safe
Brought down by my race
'Will it ever end?'

See lives lost
Hear screams of a victim
Smell the blood of the innocent
'What for?'
A piece of paper
A sick smile . . . like a tiger assaulting a bird.

We are all equal
Why choose this life?
Why be a slave of Lucifer?

'Silence.'
All is gone.
I hear footsteps. It's here.
I hide
I died

Cha-ching! Someone's five pounds richer.
Someone's alive.

Cobi Ho (13)
Churchdown School, Churchdown

There! There!

There, there, go to sleep
Share, share, not a peep
Where, where did he go?
Dare, dare, do you know?
Fair, fair, time for bed
'Care, care,' he said.
Boo!

Keeley Bishop (13)
Churchdown School, Churchdown

The Monster

What is that?
    A bird?
        A plane?
            A monster?

The hairiest thing
    You've ever seen
        With eyes that
            Glow

It stalks you
    Watching you
        Your every move
            It stares at your food

It can dig to Hell
    And
        Back

The
    Cat
        From
            Hell!

(Well, actually my nan's cat!)

Kefren Milne (13)
Churchdown School, Churchdown

The Darkness

The cold chill of the cold wind travels down my spine.
The heat of the furnace is cosy though.
But I think, what's outside, what's out there?
But I think, no, there's nothing in the darkness.
Although, what if it is the Darkness stalking me through the night?
What if it harms me or just gives me a fright?
Although I'll be safe in my room out of harm's way,
First I have to get up to my room and so I climb the stairs of doom.

I'm so close, my bedroom's in sight,
But what if something's lurking in the dark night?
But I would be safe in my room, I think.
I'm safe in my bed now, just settling down,
Until I hear a tap at the window so I get up.
I pull back the curtains to see my baby sister.
But then I remember we're on the second floor
And my sister died a year ago, so how is this so?

It was the Darkness with big red eyes and huge fangs and claws.
But I'm fine because this is what it said . . .
'I'm tired of you. I'm really bored. And since I'm through,
I think I will come after you . . . !'

James Blackshaw Dobbins (11)
Churchdown School, Churchdown

Dying London

All in the worrying
the running, running, then
safety.

Sirens moaning and the constant crying
underground.
Wrapping up for warmth as no heat in bunkers.

Suddenly when the sirens fade
the all-clear echoes through the streets of London
which are dying.

Alexander Hitchman (12)
Churchdown School, Churchdown

And There She Lay

She was my best friend.
She'd listen to my problems, she never moaned.
She always played and ran about
But then it stopped.
There she lay . . .
My best friend . . .

Her heart had stopped in the night,
Or was it just a sudden fright?
Why did she leave me?
And there she lay . . .

I miss her squeaking during the day.
I miss the wheel she ran at night.
I miss my best friend
But there she lay . . .
My best friend.

In a box, in the ground
Forever . . .
She can play
Now.

Bethany Stevens (12)
Churchdown School, Churchdown

Now And Then

I walked upon a sandy beach,
my feet as hot as fire.

> I am sitting in my rocking chair,
> In a cooled out, lonely house.

I met him on a holiday,
my heart was beating fast.

> I have no one here to talk to,
> except my tabby cat.

I walked down the aisle,
with a smile on my face.

> I am slowly drifting off
> into a midnight dream.

I had two little girls
they were everything to me.

> Now I have little time left,
> But then I had loads to spare.

Kelsey Webb (13)
Churchdown School, Churchdown

The Spiritual Jungle

Blood flows over the bare concrete ground
as a tiger bleeds in the courtyard,
where a poacher shoots his prey in the African jungle.
A screech of a hawk as its wing bleeds in harm's way
and the hawk leads the way to its spiritual life in
Animal Heaven.

A buffalo cries as its leg is trapped in a spring trap,
to die in South Africa's biggest waterhole.
The hawk leads the way to the spiritual jungle
and the buffalo is dying in the place he was born
then is flying to Heaven until dawn.

Sam Mansell (12)
Churchdown School, Churchdown

My Love For You

Sometimes I wish we were together
Just can't wait until it's us forever and ever
It's just like being young and free
No matter what, just you and me.

Another day is just another dream
With you, makes my life my reality
Can't wait till the night, lots of thoughts
But for me you're the best of all sorts.

Girl, you turn dreams into reality
With me and you, never tragedy
I just want it to be us two
I would do anything for me and you.

To be with you is a school thing
To love you is harder to sing
So I write this poem for you
To say how much I love you.

Peter Lee (14)
Churchdown School, Churchdown

Scared

Another day comes around,
Another day where I'm not safe and sound,
I shake and shiver as the door creaks open,
But what's the point in hiding?
I don't know where I'm going to be driven,
If only I hadn't been taken,
Maybe my parents wouldn't be so shaken,
But I was proud to save their lives, you see,
But that meant them taking me.
So now they are desperate to get me back,
Then I will no longer be attacked,
If we ever meet again,
I will talk of none of the pain . . .

Gemma Dooley (12)
Churchdown School, Churchdown

The Secrets

Many secrets in this place,
Some dark, some golden.
All from many trespassers and the owners,
But maybe some others.

In the basement,
Under the stairs,
In the garden
(everywhere).

From the first structure,
To the end,
The secrets will stay,
Even if they depend.

The secrets are everywhere,
You must find them.
But don't stay too long,
Or you will feel the chill . . .

James Bourke (12)
Churchdown School, Churchdown

Ghost

Every night I hear him. Every night I cry.
I've never actually seen him. I wonder if he's shy

I don't know if he is a ghost.
But is he good or bad?
Why does he make me scared?
Have I made him mad?

All the time I wonder, will he come to calm me
Or does he want to kill me?
I really want to meet him. Maybe he is near.

When I went to sleep that night . . . crash!
He is here . . .

Jess Waghorn (12)
Churchdown School, Churchdown

Haunted House

Through the door,
to the haunted house.
A creak of wood,
a squeak of a mouse.

Trees for hands,
window like eyes.
A porch for a mouth,
inside's a surprise.

The winding staircase,
leading into dark.
The roaring fire
whose ash leaves a mark.

Out of the door,
to the haunted house.
No more creaking wood.
No more squeaking mouse.

Callum Dawson-Williams (11)
Churchdown School, Churchdown

Crying Forever

She cried all day and she cried all night,
Hoping that someone would hear her.
But no one heard her,
No one cared,
No one knew that she was there.
But she was. Left to die.
Until someone heard her frantic cries
And came to rescue her.
He looked and looked for the crying girl
But he couldn't find her,
Although he did find a cracked mirror
With tears running down . . .

Lauren McLean (12)
Churchdown School, Churchdown

Crystal Clear

Hi, I'm Crystal Clear
Can't you hear?
I'm silky blue
And silver too
But best of all I glisten in the moonlight
Shine a light on the purple-faced kite

I freeze when it's cold
Like stage fright when bold
I melt when it's warm
Like a breeze in the morn
Because I'm Crystal Clear
I know you can hear

Sooo
Let's shimmer
Aawwaayy!

Chloe-May Barton (13)
Churchdown School, Churchdown

Dan The Man And His Ice Cream Van

Dan the man and his ice cream van
always serve the same old man.
As he drove he saw Blueberry Grove
and he went on down
from his ice cream van to town
where he saw the same old man,
but Dan the man and his ice cream van
went down through this dark, dark town,
into the coldest creepiest park,
where there was a girl who called him Earl.
Next time you drive, make sure you thrive
upon the innocence of all.
Dan the man and his ice cream van
always served the same . . . old . . . man.

Henry Noble (12)
Churchdown School, Churchdown

If I Had A Horse

If I had a horse we would be,
Best of friends, my horse and me.

Sitting on her back, the wind in my hair,
Faster and faster our journey we'd share.
Free in a world of our own,
Happier times never been known.

The sound of her hooves as we'd ride along,
As you listen carefully, they'd sing a song.

Over the fields into the stream,
Into the meadow where no one has been.

If I had a horse, we would be
Best of friends, my horse and me.

Alice Jones (12)
Churchdown School, Churchdown

My Dog Molly

I love the way you eat my Scalextric
And when you jump in our game of cricket
How you walk over my work books with muddy feet
Just for a stroke
To you this would be an annoying dog
But to me she is a special dog

Given the chance you would take out the postman
But instead, you rip up our mail
Squirrels have no chance as you chase them around
To you this would be an annoying dog
But to me she is a special dog

Footballers, red with rage, as you steal their ball and score a goal
Bark at anything and pull on your lead
Roll on Mum's daffodils and get plastered in mud
To you this would be an annoying dog
But to me she is a special dog!

Daniel Bristow (12)
Cornwallis Academy, Maidstone

No Man's Land

War, war
Bombs, bangs
Screams, shrieks
Bodies strewn across
No man's land
Guns, grenades
Death parade
Funerals galore
Wounds, weeping
Blood, bruises
Shells, shrapnel
In No man's land

War, war
Trenches, tanks
Skies grow cloudy, ashes fall
Tears by families, shared by all

How many planes shot down?
How many soldiers died?
Think of their mothers, their children, their wives
Every moment seems like forever
As off they go to say goodbye,
As the funeral car goes by
They cry for him who died
Sun comes out, shining bright
To take my son towards the light.
His soul emerges from his body,
Floating gracefully to his Heaven.

Every night I pray to him,
My son, a husband, a dad
He hears my gentle whispers,
I hear his reply,
I feel he's sitting near me,
Watching my every move.

If only I could see my darling son
For one last time,
For me to say my goodbyes.

Katie Bishop (14) & Amber Kirk (13)
Cornwallis Academy, Maidstone

You're My Best Friend

I once was lonely,
No one to talk to.
But then a miracle came,
And it had to be you.

She's corny and cheesy,
But that's OK.
She's loving and caring,
Every night and day.

She makes me laugh,
And she's a little bit mad.
But she's there for me,
When I'm feeling sad.

We're always giggling,
Dying of laughter.
We both like a story,
With a 'happily ever after'.

We've never fallen out,
Not now, not ever.
We're always there for each other,
Whatever the weather.

I once was lonely,
But now I'm found.
I've now got a friend,
To pick me up from the ground.

Jazmin Qunta & Kirsty Russell (14)
Cornwallis Academy, Maidstone

My Mum

Mum, you mean the world to me,
You are precious and so sweet,
You are very kind and helpful,
You mean everything to me.

Mum, if you were a flower,
You would be the biggest one there,
I would pick you,
Because you are my one and only mum.

You tiptoe into our bedrooms,
To kiss us all goodnight,
And say that silly saying, 'Don't let the bedbugs bite.'

Mum, you are wonderful,
I hope I grow up like you,
Caring, honest and beautiful too,
I love you now and forever.

Mum, you are a treasure,
And I love you so,
You are always there for us,
And I wish for you to know,
You are one in a million,
And your hugs always show,
I really love you dearly, now everyone will know.

Bethany Carreras (12)
Cornwallis Academy, Maidstone

Don't Give Up

When you're all alone, don't give up
When there's no one there, don't give up
When you're down for the count, don't give up
When there is no hope in the jaws of defeat, don't give up
When all you have is hope, never give up
Because when you never give up
You will rise and rise again and lambs will become lions.

Jacob Andreassen (12)
Cornwallis Academy, Maidstone

The New Boy

I feel sorry for the new boy
He's all by himself
Sitting there, judging us or simply observing.
He sits there every day with a mournful look
A look I wish I could take away
If only I could.

I feel sorry for the new boy
Oh the people I meet
If only he could share them too, make friends.
He guards the bench he's perched on
Scared to let anyone in
If only he could.

I feel sorry for the new boy
He seems really sweet
However no one sees what I see.
He has no friends, no company except a little girl
A girl who will introduce herself
Only because . . .
She feels sorry for the new boy
Oh the poor new boy
She feels sorry for the new boy
The people he shall meet.

Elaine Kemp (14)
Cornwallis Academy, Maidstone

True Friends

My friends are loud
And make me proud.
They don't boast
When I need them most.
They are really pretty
Just like a kitty.
That makes me know
That they will never go.

Ellie Wyatt (12)
Cornwallis Academy, Maidstone

Friends

Friends are not just people,
They are a shimmering light which we look up to,
I trust my friends,
And they trust me,

Friends are things that we must look after,
Through thick and thin,
We are all still full of laughter,
When time is at its worst,
You are there for me,
And that's what means most,

You believe everything I say,
You make me happy throughout the day,
And there for me whenever I need you,

So there I have it,
My perfect friend,
You're funny,
Gullible,
There for me,
But most of all, you are loyal,
The one thing that you possess,
That no one else on this planet can.

Jack French (12)
Cornwallis Academy, Maidstone

Friends

Friends, friends, friends,
Friends are funny.
Friends are there when you have a bad thing up your back.
Friends make you happy not sad,
Friends are there next to you, behind you.
Friends are there because there are friends for you.
Friends, friends, friends.

Angus Knowler (12)
Cornwallis Academy, Maidstone

A True Friend Is . . .

Someone you can talk to,
Someone who will keep your secrets,
Someone who will never leave,
And someone who will take care of you!

A swish of a tail,
A happy kicker,
An eager stomp of a hoof,
The elation in my face.

There's my friend,
With crystal-blue eyes,
A silky, shiny, shimmering, cream coat,
With a neatly combed mane and tail,
Like an angel,

My friend,
My horse,
The one I love
And will treasure,
For ever and ever.

Billie Allbury-Smith (12)
Cornwallis Academy, Maidstone

What Is It?

It's fluffy and white,
and can bite.
It stands on four legs,
and sometimes begs.
It chews on a bone,
it plays with toys
and it's a boy.
It's cuddly and warm,
and lots are born.
What is it?

A: A dog!

Lianna Wallace (13)
Cornwallis Academy, Maidstone

Friendship

Friendship is the best
I would like to say the rest,
Empty feelings are the worst
So come out and burst,
Laughter is the light in me
So let yourself be free,
Shine like a star
And you can go very far,
We are always there for each other
Forever, till the end,
Because this girl right here
Is my best friend.
She has been right here forever
From the start,
My best friend is a work of art.
We have had so much laughter and fun,
Until I shot her with a gun.
I regret what I've done,
We had so much fun!

Laura Wells & Amie Chattenton (14)
Cornwallis Academy, Maidstone

My Dog

My dog is small
My dog is round
She makes a flip-floppy sound

My dog has fur as white as snow
My dog likes her pink bow

My dog is curly
Her feet are quite furry

My dog might get cold
But she always has a heart of gold.

I love you Jess.

Charlotte Lavender (13)
Cornwallis Academy, Maidstone

If I Could

If I could
Play sport,
Be fit and strong,
I would be liked.

If I could
Run like the wind,
Have stamina and power,
I could be in the Olympics.

If I could
Be smart,
Have a good job with money,
I would be successful.

But I'm not and I can't.
I'm me!

Michael Welbourne (12)
Cornwallis Academy, Maidstone

Together

Breakfast, lunch and dinner,
Sitting at the table together,
Eating for ages,
No chatting, the last time was before sunset

Driving around the town,
Gazing for shops that we need to go to,
A restaurant that lights up as much
As the sun does in the morning.

At home in the garden,
On the hottest day of the year,
Paddling pool out and gently drifting around.

At the end of the day we sit down together
And think how lucky we are to have a family.

Hannah Tyler (12)
Cornwallis Academy, Maidstone

If You Call Me

If you call me once, I will be right there.
If you call me twice, I know that you care.

If you ever leave me, I don't know what I'd do.
But once I see that note right there, I know that it's true.

Walking down the street, confused out of my mind.
I always treated you nicely, I was always kind.

If you were by my side,
My fears would never have to hide.

But seeing as you're not here,
I guess I'm going to have to fear.

But I know I've got my friends forever.
But instead of you, I've always got them through whatever.

Adam Shallcross (13)
Cornwallis Academy, Maidstone

A Day On A Sunny Beach

As people walk past
On a bright sunny day
The luscious green grass
The sand golden as hay
The thoughtless littering
Children playing
I watch the bright sun glittering
While I hear everyone saying
'The sun is dying'
Everyone going
Kids tired and crying
Cars with caravans towing
From crashing seas to frothing foam
The bronzed sun worshippers slowly return home.

Paige Souten (12)
Cornwallis Academy, Maidstone

The Performer

You are next,
Heart pounding,
Mind racing,
Wondering what they are going to think of you,
Your eyes scan the room,
Staring at the audience,
Trying to read their expressions,
You talk,
They laugh,
You laugh,
Walk off the stage,
Out of the room,
You smile,
They like you!

Aimee Miller (12)
Cornwallis Academy, Maidstone

What Is It?

It's fluffy and brown
hops around.
Stands on four legs
and chews all my pegs.
It sleeps in a cage
whilst eating hay.
They're friendly and warm
as soon as they're born.
It kicks up the hay
as soon as it lays.
It eats lots of carrots.
What is it?

A: A rabbit!

Gemma Lawrance (13)
Cornwallis Academy, Maidstone

The Concert

All around you people screaming.
People waving.
People shouting.
The curtain opens.
They're screaming louder.
They stop screaming.
Onstage they are singing.
More screaming.
Curtain closing.
Concert done.

Lauren Butler (12)
Cornwallis Academy, Maidstone

My Family

My mummy is a person who comforts me at night
she helps me with nightmares, she is my light.

My brother is a person who is fabulous and fun
but when he annoys me I kick him up the bum!

My dad is a person who is tall and strong
and you will often find he is never wrong.

The same with my sister, she is very smart
but now it's time to just look into your heart.

Toby Patey-Ford
Cornwallis Academy, Maidstone

Love

You say that you only fall in love once in a lifetime,
with butterflies dancing around your stomach.
You say my heartbeat lies within your chest.
You say you will take my heart and put it next to yours
as long as we are meant to be.
You say you will take my love and mix it with yours
until the sun goes cold.
You say you wrote your name in my heart,
Forever it may stay.

Emma Clark (14)
Cornwallis Academy, Maidstone

A Love Poem

My love for you is like a rose,
as each passing day, it grows and grows,
until high in the sky.

My love for you is like climbing a tree,
I look up and see a heart-shaped cloud
of you and me.

Molly Palmer (12)
Cornwallis Academy, Maidstone

The Daffodils

The daffodils
Are blowing in the wind
God's pushing them
The yellow petals
The silky petals under
The big blue sky.

Charlotte Pursey (12)
Cornwallis Academy, Maidstone

Autumn Days

The clouds move swiftly in the light blue sky,
The sun up high shines bright with perceptive shine,
And the howling wind rushes past,
While the rain falls down with ease,
And the birds fly around singing in the trees,
But the moon rolls on while the day goes by.

Charley Bray (11)
Cornwallis Academy, Maidstone

Now You're Gone!

You're here with me.
You will never leave me.
Your love and mine is strong.
Even though you're far away
Your love is always with me
In my heart.

Now you're gone
I realise that I can't live
Without you.
I need you back
But you're never coming back
You can't.

You had a problem with your heart.
My heart is now destroyed
But your memories
Are always with me.

Rebecca Harding (14)
Denefield School, Tilehurst

Just Because

Just because I have not broken a bone in my body,
It doesn't mean I am not dangerous.

Just because I hate walking,
It doesn't mean I don't like running.

Just because I hate reading,
It doesn't mean I hate pictures.

Just because I hate rugby,
It doesn't mean I hate other sport.

Shawni James Vickery (11)
Denefield School, Tilehurst

The World

The world is a kind and nice place for us,
The world has lovely doctors and nurses to look after us,
The world has good schools and places for us to learn,
The world has food for us to live,
The world has lovely gifts and toys for us to play with,
The world has got beautiful trees and landscapes,
The world has lots of history within it,
The world has different football teams but England is the best,
The world is trying to be green to protect the world.

Laura Szandrowycz (11)
Denefield School, Tilehurst

My Poem

I wake up every Monday to Friday, every hard day.
Detentions or no detentions, still a hard day.
I am trying to do my best
Outside can be racist, no place for me.
3pm, happy time for me.
At home, parents are at home.

Tobiasz Nadworny (12)
Denefield School, Tilehurst

Fish

F ish swimming in the sea.
I f only I could catch one for my tea.
S alt and vinegar on my meal.
H ow happy that will make me feel.

Samara Edwards (11)
Denefield School, Tilehurst

The Tragic Story Of Tom Mullaney

Coldness dawned upon my heart
As I read the threats online
I sat there in silence as my life fell apart
No one knew how I really felt as I just said I was fine.

Every day I found some more
Threats that messed with my mind
And with every knock at the door
I thought of courage I wish I could find

They made me very stressed
They said they would beat me at school
They made me feel depressed
They drove me too far, they thought they were cool

I was in tears the day before
I wish they would leave me alone
I just couldn't take anymore
The pressure had just grown

Wednesday was the day I blew
Everything I tried had failed
I wanted my life to be new
I was in tears and I know I shouldn't but I bailed.

The moral of this story is never bully
It can drive people further than you think.

Lucy Meilack (12)
Heathfield Community College, Heathfield

Stieg Larsson
(In memory of Stieg Larsson, who died 9th November 2004)

Stieg Larsson was just a new beginner,
He dreamt that he would become a winner,
He was just starting his career,
And he stepped in with no fear.

He began writing his first book ever,
And made it all extremely clever,
Stieg Larsson came up with the most complicated themes,
And finally someone answered all his dreams.

A beginning journalist with a Swedish background,
He wrote and he wrote, all the time waiting to be found,
When his first book was published Stieg was over the moon,
He was excited about writing a new one soon.

He began to write his second book ever,
And made it all extremely clever,
Stieg Larsson came up with the most complicated themes,
And finally someone answered all his dreams.

When Stieg Larsson published his second book,
People didn't take a second look,
But little did the Swedish author know,
His book would be one hell of a great show!

He began to write his third book ever,
And made it all extremely clever,
Stieg Larsson came up with the most complicated themes,
And finally someone answered all his dreams.

In 2004 something fatal came,
Stieg Larsson would never make it to fame,
A heart attack took his life away,
He was pronounced dead, to much dismay.

In 2010 he had his first film made,
A tribute that everyone felt had to be paid,
The books became famous in 2008,
But unfortunately for Stieg, it was just too late.

I suppose you're wondering, 'Where are his cash notes?'
The answer to that question is, they are now his folks,
Larsson's partner forever,
Won't get a penny, not ever.

In a way, Larsson and van Gogh are the same,
The fact that they never got to see their fame,
Larsson never got to enjoy his moment of glory,
And that, folks, is the end of my story.

Elly Ambridge (13)
Heathfield Community College, Heathfield

The Iceland Volcano

'Twas the spring of the year 2010
An age when folk travelled afar.
Planes were the favoured transport of men
Faster than boat, train or car.

High in the north a volcano erupted
Spewing fire and rock, smoke and ash
Which left these people lost and stranded
Costing the airlines plenty of cash

Cash was the oil greasing the engine
Of a world obsessed with possession and wealth.
The chaos resulting, as you can imagine,
Was a strain on everyone's emotional health

The stress was driving everyone crazy
Due to the fact the planes couldn't fly.
The pilots' vision was worse than hazy
So planes were unable to take to the sky

Now that the ash has cleared away
The planes have returned to the air
Which means we're able to now go on holiday;
The only bad news is the cost of the fare!

Alex von Barnholt (13)
Heathfield Community College, Heathfield

Only Once

Down she went,
Quick as a flash.
Only once she looked,
And that cost her dearly.

She was only fourteen,
She was only going home.
Only once she looked,
And that cost her dearly.

The woman didn't notice the girl,
And the girl didn't notice the car.
Only once she looked,
And that cost her dearly.

They closed the road for an hour,
While everyone tried to help.
Only once she looked,
And that cost her dearly.

Her injuries were so severe,
She was airlifted to hospital.
Only once she looked,
And that cost her dearly.

Taken to Kent & Sussex hospital,
With a suspected fractured skull.
Only once she looked,
And that cost her dearly.

Later she was moved to a hospital in London,
As she needed much more help.
Only once she looked,
And that cost her dearly.

She ended up in intensive care,
In Great Ormond Street Hospital.
Only once she looked,
And that cost her dearly.

Her injuries were severe,
But not life-threatening.
Only once she looked,
And that cost her dearly.

Now I'm sure you've learnt a lesson,
And I'm sure so has she.
Only once she looked,
And that cost her dearly.

Jessica Kraft (12)
Heathfield Community College, Heathfield

The Story Of Joe

Joe Townsend, a 20-year-old
His life had been turned very cold.
Everything has changed and there's no pain
Although memories still remain.

Fighting for his country, fighting every day
Suddenly an explosion took his legs away.
Everything has changed and there's no pain
Although memories still remain.

He travels home to find those he loves
His grandparents relieved that he wasn't sent above.
Everything has changed and there's no pain
Although memories still remain.

Even though disabled he still wanted to live
So a bungalow was what his grandparents wanted to give.
Everything has changed and there's no pain
Although memories still remain.

To build it in the garden was what they planned
They didn't see a problem as it was their land.
Everything has changed and there's no pain
Although memories still remain.

The council denied planning permission
And they were disappointed with that decision.
Everything has changed and there's no pain
Although memories still remain.

Many people thought this was wrong
So they decided to protest for however long.
Everything has changed and there's no pain
Although memories still remain.

After a battle that was won
The building of the bungalow could be done.
Everything has changed and there's no pain
Although memories still remain.

So after this journey through this difficult maze
His life is explained in this one phrase.
'Everything has changed and there's no pain
Although memories still remain'.

Sophie-Rose McDonagh (12)
Heathfield Community College, Heathfield

Apart At Last . . . But Together Forever

Days go past when we were as one,
Our actions the same,
Our lives were done,
Hand in hand all the way,
Tiny miracles day by day.

Outsiders from the rest,
That is what we were,
A complete and utter mess,
Tiny miracles day by day.

It's time to change,
That's what our parents say,
We have to now rearrange,
Tiny miracles day by day.

14 hour op, that's quite a lot,
If that means we'll become individual,
How can we say not,
Tiny miracles day by day.

I now see my brother,
Lying next to me,
Part of another,
Tiny miracles day by day.

My parents now say, they're as happy as ever,
Now two have become one,
Apart at last but . . . together forever,
Tiny miracles day by day.

Emily Simpson (13)
Heathfield Community College, Heathfield

Conjoined Twins

Right from the start,
Even from their tiny hearts,
Apart at last
Together always.

Friends forever,
Their friendship as tight as leather,
Apart at last
Together always.

Only until the doctor realised they were joined chest to chest,
Their mother cradled her babies and hoped for the best
Apart at last
Together always.

So they came up with a plan,
To in fourteen hours separate the twins
Apart at last
Together always.

How delighted was the mother,
When she saw she had two children who weren't conjoined
Apart at last
Together always.

Even through the pain and suffering,
Her twins were toughening
Apart at last
Together always.

So the mother took her babies home,
And thought about what an amazing life her children would have
Apart at last
Together always.

Leyla Owen (13)
Heathfield Community College, Heathfield

Don't Mind Me, I Live Here
(This can be sung to the tune of 'Sing A Song of Sixpence')

When the regal peacock,
Perches in the tree,
People often stop to ask,
Whether he belongs to me.

When he struts around his kingdom,
He often beckons me,
To let you know that,
It must be time for tea.

When he comes into my kitchen,
With arrogance sits on the sink,
His exotic tail feathers shining,
Then sits there with a blink.

When it gets to morning,
He's awake at break of dawn,
To sing and wake up everyone,
With a massive yawn.

You should never ignore him,
Otherwise he turns into a snob,
If you dare say the 'no' word,
He'll peck you and it throbs.

I bet you're sitting thinking,
Why don't you shoo him away?
The reply I often give is,
'I'd rather he just stayed.'

Skye Ostermeyer (13)
Heathfield Community College, Heathfield

Government

Out of the picture perspective
too, the media's eyes are shut and closed
and so Gordon Brown is out of town!

A hung parliament is in the air
future uncertainties for many there, then
out of the blue David Cameron
turns up too.

The Lib Dems are lost and done
and they haven't won, they
have done a deal and got second
place but Labour's out of the race.

There's a fight now for Labour's
crown, up and down
counties squabbling here, there
and everywhere.

They're having a party at our expense
laughing and joking, that's definitely
not immense, unhappy we are with our
parliament's pretence!

Jess Douglas (13)
Heathfield Community College, Heathfield

Friends

Friends are like gold,
The old and the new.
Wherever you go,
They will go too.
True friends are like brothers -
They stand by your side,
They stay with you every inch of the ride.
You're so close, you're glued together.
One thing's for sure, true friends are forever.

Richard Crawley (12)
Highcrest Community School, High Wycombe

My Teddy

When I sleep in the wintry night,
I hear struggles like a fight.
My teddy in my arms as soft as a pillow,
smiling as we dream about food, friends, and sitting by the willows!
It isn't very comfortable,
the bed, rigid, icy and wet.
But we still lie in the dark,
scared, lonely,
and filled with darkening dread.

I miss my mummy who left one day,
she was sent to the showers to fetch her pay!
But now I know why she went to stay.
The truth has hit me in the face.
Smack!
That's what it felt like that night I lay.
They work us hard, beat us, and mistreat us,
Why had I and Teddy believed in such a thing?

Today it's my turn in the shower,
after finishing work I delay and cower.
As I strip off my clothes, my body bruised and battered,
the room is silver, and littered, the mirror is shattered!
The room hurt me inside,
like a broken heart struck with grief,
betrayal,
and downright terror.

Now I ask you to recall as Teddy falls to the floor,
the way they killed, disregarded and treated us,
everyone should remember so it won't happen again,
remember the heartache, and remember the pain.
I was a Jew filled with glee,
but tonight the Nazis murdered me!

Darrian George-Johnson (12)
Highcrest Community School, High Wycombe

The Voices

The voices talk to me
And tell me what they see;
Tell me what they think of my face
Tell me what they think of my race,
I just want them to go away!

The voices talk to me
And tell me what they see;
They call my face dirty and black
They call my face ugly, in fact,
I just want them to go away!

The voices talk to me
And tell me what they see;
They say I don't belong
They say that I being born, was wrong,
I just want them to go away!

It's time to stop!
Stop those cruel voices -
There's only one way,
Only one way to make them pay:
To tell!

Xyla Jacobs (12)
Highcrest Community School, High Wycombe

Clowns

They make you laugh, they make you cry,
They end the show, they say goodbye;
But they never stop smiling.

If you are scared, you scream and shout
If you love them you jump about;
But they never stop smiling.

They love to joke and bounce around,
Their cheeks are red, their noses are round;
But they never stop smiling.

You go to bed, you have bad dreams,
A smiley clown: never all that seems;
But they never stop smiling.

They smile and smile all day and night,
It freaks you out, it gives you a fright;
They don't know when to stop smiling.

They're in your house, they're in your bed,
They're under the covers, they're in your head;
And they never stop smiling.

Caity Hicks (12)
Highcrest Community School, High Wycombe

Missing!

I search in and out of the empty rooms,
looking for a clue,
I search in and out of the empty rooms,
looking for something to do.
Searching in and out of the empty rooms,
no objects do I find,
Searching in and out of the empty rooms,
looking for a rhyme.
And now I've found my pretty pattern,
weaving through the air,
I spin and turn and smile and flutter,
finally starting to care.
I turn around and see it's there, just there,
what I've been looking for,
It's actually hanging there, there,
on the old wooden door.
I've found the missing object,
the thing I can't live without,
It's pink all right, it's shining bright,
it's my brain without a doubt!

Emma Prince (12)
Highcrest Community School, High Wycombe

Alone!

Alone!
On an island:
Sand blowing in my face, blinding me.
Wind so strong it sweeps me off my feet,
The salty ocean air hypnotising me,
Wishing someone would come and whisk me away!
Sun so hot I wither.
Birds sit on me all day pecking at my neck,
Monkeys eating away at my last and only food.
Hungry for company, someone to talk to.

Aeroplanes fly over my head, so high they can't see me.
As if a dot on the horizon!
My brothers and sisters were chopped down,
Now they're hotel roofs.
Mixed emotions sad, angry and lonely,
Isolated.
Will I ever be free?
It's a very hard life in what people would call . . .
Paradise!

Charlotte Louise Helene Lawrence (12)
Highcrest Community School, High Wycombe

I Want To Live The World For Someone

I want to live the world for someone,
so my life can have some meaning, many meanings
someone that I can love and trust,
and that will always be there
to help, trust and guide me, forever,
through one life to the next.

Savage winds and waves will bash the cliff-side wall,
but they will never prevail, not this time
for they are much weaker,
weaker than our need for one another,
the need that is bound with the tightest string, the string of love,
that will never break or split.

I want to live the world for someone,
show them the universe, my universe
and all the colours and sounds in it;
and I want to take their hand in mine,
so that we can walk side by side,
down this path called 'life'.

Charlie Basham (12)
Highcrest Community School, High Wycombe

The Night

The moon shines bright,
in the night.
The dark starry sky attracts animals and tiny life,
in the night.
Silence replaces the noise of the day,
in the night.
The streetlights become the sun,
of the night.
We all get sent off to dreamland
in the night.
Peace at last.
I love the night.

Jeremiah Patel (11)
Highcrest Community School, High Wycombe

I Wonder Why

I wonder why stars fill the sky?
Silver and glittering,
Never seen such a thing,
So brightly shining,
The sight's better than anything.
Stars fill the sky,
In wonder why stars fill the sky?
Thousands and thousands of little sparkles,
Tiny little glimmering balls,
Just looking down on me; ever so bright,
Giving me light through the night.
Stars fill the sky,
I wonder why stars fill the sky?

Olivia Sutherland (12)
Highcrest Community School, High Wycombe

That Little Bird

That little bird with its breast so bright
Gave my cat a little fright.

As he landed on my window sill
I thought to myself, oh, what a thrill.

To see him there
With love and care.

The bird so close to me
Nearly landed in my tea.

That little bird with its breast so bright
Off he flew into the night.

Dannii Laine (12)
Highcrest Community School, High Wycombe

Holding On

In the past I've made mistakes,
Done things I now regret,
But you accepted me without doubt,
And I was so thankful for that.

But when I was seven you died,
And I was there to see it,
It broke my heart finding out,
That your voice had disappeared,
You smile would never surface,
And your heart would never beat.

Although they told me I had to rest,
I ran away from them,
From the crying and the groaning,
The living and the dead.

I don't know where I went,
And I don't know when they found me,
But when I woke again,
I was in my familiar bed,
Back in a familiar room,
Back in my bedroom again.

I thought it was all a dream,
But I was covered in cuts,
Scars that would never heal,
Like the cuts placed in my heart.

You were gone to a faraway place,
A place I could never reach,
I will not see you again,
Not until I die.

The nightmares almost killed me,
The shock made me ill,
The depression made me sick,
What is this I feel?

When you left the world was sad,
I couldn't do anything,
I missed you so bad,

That last promise I made to you,
I couldn't keep,
What should I do?

You died in a car crash,
In which I survived,
The van couldn't stop,
It was going to fast.

Now almost seven years later,
I have found a way,
To live my life,
Is that okay?

Just remember we miss you,
But you won't be lonely for long,
I will come and see you,
I will try to be strong.

Shannon Johnson (13)
Holywells High School, Ipswich

Trapped

Trapped in school,
Day after day,
My voice on high,
Screaming inside,
I'm trapped,
The door's locked,
My pen won't stop,
Pages are filled,
Ink stains are blue,
The sky's bright,
Oh please don't make me feel blue,
That's the bell,
Ring, ring, ring,
Smiles on everything,
All my friends waiting outside,
Freedom's here to take its line.

Katie Chaplin (11)
Holywells High School, Ipswich

Stronger!

Don't make fun of me
It's so not fair
I would rather stay home alone
I don't care.

Teachers might like me
And I might get good grades
It gets you a long way
My parents always say.

So what if I stay in rather than go out?
So what if I'm not popular?
The friends I do have really count.

I might walk away from trouble,
I might think before I act
But one of these days I just might crack.

The pressure you put on me
Is ruining my life
But somehow every name, slap and push
Makes me stronger inside
Gives me courage to stand up to you
And fight back.

I'm getting stronger
Less scared by the night
Making fun of me
Does you no good
You need to back off.

Months go by
I don't care
You made my life hell
So bad that I couldn't breathe
I used to come home crying every night
Now I come home happy.

Looking back now
I don't know why you picked on me
Because in the end I've turned out better than you
I have achieved my dreams

Got even more maybe
So as you walk by me in the street
Just think if you might have been like me
You might have everything

I have a great job
An expensive car
I can afford designer clothes
And most importantly
I have someone who loves me for who I am.
Who loves me enough to respect me
Who is not afraid to walk down the street with me
Unlike you.

Shannon Sewell (13)
Holywells High School, Ipswich

Childhood!

Childhood is a memory everybody forgets
Childhood is a song that never ends
Childhood I will never forget because all of the
happiness is my childhood.

But childhood doesn't last forever, nothing does
My life is a whole other tale
Like a snail trail
Keeps going and going and never stops
My life goes up and down
Some bad days, some good days
Like no other
Meeting new people
Making new friends, but love is something
That mends everything.

Childhood has gone, a new start has just begun
Waiting for the next day that will leave the meeting of tomorrow.

Chelsea Chatfield (12)
Holywells High School, Ipswich

A Day At School

A te a bacon roll and shortbread at break.
B ounced the ball so high.
C aught the ball.
D ropped my phone.
E ntered the classroom.
F orgot my homework.
G ot a ten-minute break.
H eard my friend getting shouted at.
I njured my foot.
J umped in PE.
K nocked on the door so I could go in.
L ost my homework.
M ade a frame in DT.
N oticed my phone was at home.
O pened the door.
P ulled the chair to me.
Q ueued up in the lunch hall.
R an as fast as I could in PE
S at down in lunch.
T alked to my friends all day.
U nderstood my teacher.
V olunteered my friend in PE.
W as bored all day.
X -rays were what we looked at in science.
Y elled my friend's name.
Z ipped my coat up.

Candice Sobers (11)
Holywells High School, Ipswich

Young Love

Love for the young can be very cute
But other times it can be very poop.
Say sometimes you can be happy,
But other times you can still be broken,
If I say that I'm happy, will you believe me?

Nothing in the world can change the way you love,
But can you change it in your heart?
Or are you as strong as a dove?

Are you orange or pink?
Or fresh, or stink?
Tell me now, or leave me forever,
Can you tell me 'cause I need to know,
Everything about you just makes me glow.

Can you keep this secret that I love you,
Or does this moment stay forever to stalk you?
You only have two,
That I shall keep, just hold that thought,
This is too deep.

Could you love me forever, and a billion times more than I ask?
Could you be there for me, for whenever it's hard?
Could you be here and comfort me,
And tell me you hurt me?
And hugs and kisses,
Can you not see?

Eloise Wells (13)
Holywells High School, Ipswich

A Day At School

A te an apple.
B ounced a ball.
C aught a fly when I yawned.
D ozed off in a maths lesson.
E xplained the answer to my friend.
F orgot my homework.
G rumbled yesterday.
H omework, didn't do it
I gnored my teacher's instructions.
J oked around with my friends.
K icked a can around the playground.
L aughed at Liam's joke.
M ade some chocolate.
N agged at Liam.
O pened the door.
P layed football.
Q uizzed my friends on their homework.
R an with my friend.
S at on a chair.
T ried to do my work.
U nderstood the teacher.
V olunteered to collect.
W aited for the bell.

Owen Lander (12)
Holywells High School, Ipswich

Sins Of Our Fathers

All the time, fire and death,
Are we all that is left?
The war was declared by the lost generation,
But yet it is ours that suffer its detonation.
The sins of our fathers,
When will they end?
Will all this suffering be the next trend?

They speak of guilt and of having no choice,
So no one knows their hands are moist.
The blood of our soldiers,
It lies on their conscience.

Will our deaths ever have meaning?
Or will the souls of our sons,
Be the ones that need healing?

Will the sins of our fathers become our sins too?
They say they are sorry,
But this is not true.
Will no one ask about the deaths of our crew?
What is that noise?
Did they make their choice?

Ryan Allington (12)
Holywells High School, Ipswich

Everlasting Love

You may not even notice me when I see you on the street,
But your love is so enchanting, boy, it sweeps me off my feet.

Thing is, I need you much more than the oxygen we breathe,
You stole my heart and broke it like a robber or a thief.

Finding you again is like finding a teardrop in the ocean,
I'm lost without you, got me all hooked up on this love potion.

This love is everlasting and you've given it a meaning,
To feel your kiss, I wouldn't miss, but I'd only be dreaming.

Ellen Day (13)
Holywells High School, Ipswich

I Am Onica

I am Onica and this is me
I am Onica, can't you see?
Sometimes I want to shout,
Tell everyone what I'm about.
But I don't have the strength to let it out.

I am Onica and this is me.
I am Onica, can't you see?
I try and try
But I'm too shy.
The voice is locked inside of me.

I am Onica and this is me
I am Onica, can't you see?
Do you have a key
To open me
To see my insides?

Onica Hussain (12)
Holywells High School, Ipswich

Miracles

You are like a miracle to me,
You're always there when I need you,
My friends are like miracles to me,
My family are my miracles,
Miracles are when you are walking to school
And you can smell the fresh grown grass,
Miracles are when you're playing with your friends, having fun,
Miracles are when you are playing with your pet
Stroking their soft fur,
A miracle is when you're lying in your bed,
Thinking of that special person,
When I see you, you are like a miracle to me,
I may not be a miracle to you,
But you are my miracle.

Chloe Wright (12)
Holywells High School, Ipswich

Can You Guess?

Some are bouncy, some are happy
Some are quiet, some are yappy
They can be vicious, they can be sweet
They can jump up and knock you off your feet
They can be big, they can be small
They can cause trouble or not at all
They can be short, they can be long
Their name can be used in a song
They can be fat, they can be thin
They can make a lot of din
They can be kind and very nice
I just need one that will suffice
I wrote this all in just one font
But can you guess what it is I want?

A: A dog.

Devon Old-Gooch (13)
Holywells High School, Ipswich

Baby Love

I am 100% sure this is love.
People say love ain't the same when you're young.
Baby, when times are hard, push comes to shove.
Can you remember the first time I rung?

You always did wear a bit too much glossy,
I don't know why 'cause you were always a stunner.
You will always be at the top of my possé.
Me and you Babe, together forever.

When I stare into your beautiful eyes,
Well Baby, I just get hypnotised.
And it's not much of a surprise.
I know I told you all those lies.

But my baby girl, I love you long times,
I'm not just saying it because it rhymes.

Warren Curtis (12)
Holywells High School, Ipswich

Baby I Love You

Baby, I love you, you're my everything,
Your eyes are like stars in the midnight sky,
When I saw you the bells started to ring,
You're always here and your love has me high.

Baby, you're special, I would cry for you,
Our love burns like a fire in the night,
Give me a chance and I will die for you,
Our love is taking off, prepare for flight.

Baby, it's so real I think this is love,
Can't you feel it? It's obvious you do,
It's like baby Cupid sent from above,
I really love you, do you love me too?

I would just like to say I love you loads,
My token of love, please accept this rose.

Laura Bowen (13)
Holywells High School, Ipswich

Football Sonnet

There are England fans that are football mad,
I hope my dad does a bet on Lampard,
I think football hooligans are so sad,
Hopefully there will not be any red cards.

I really, really hope that England win,
We've definitely got an okay chance,
My grandad will be watching with some gin,
They better do well, it's not a fun dance.

Hopefully we will be lifting the Cup,
Let's all hope they get led to victory,
Then our FIFA world ranking will go up,
Hopefully they can repeat history.

If England don't win for the second time,
I have wasted time by doing this rhyme.

Jack Podd (12)
Holywells High School, Ipswich

I Don't Care!

I used to be blonde, didn't mean I was dumb.
I used to hate people moaning about my looks.
I used to think 'cause I wasn't that pretty, it didn't mean
you could judge me.
I never was the skinniest girl, doesn't mean I'm not a good person.
I never was the prettiest girl, doesn't mean you can judge me.
I never was the kindest girl, doesn't mean I'm still horrible.
Now I'm getting older, I don't care what people think of me.
You can judge me, it will hurt deep down.
You can judge me, I'll try and show I really don't care.
You can judge me, isn't up people for what I look like and who I am.
I'm just an ordinary girl,
I'm just the same as I used to be.
I am . . . just the same as you!

Chloe Adams (12)
Holywells High School, Ipswich

Life

When you were little you planned your life,
Chose what job you wanted,
And how many kids you were going to have.

But life isn't as simple as you planned it,
First you have to get past the bullies,
Then find who your best friends are,
Also you have to get the grades.

That seems simple but when you live it
It really isn't,
When I'm a big success,
I'm going to look down at the people who misjudged me
And laugh as they struggle by,
That's just life!

Toni Maria Abrahams (12)
Holywells High School, Ipswich

I Was Young

I was young,
I didn't know any better,
How life would change me.
I wasn't aware.
I lived a blissful childhood which soon drained away.
Now I'm older, going through changes,
Death, family, friends and me.
Changing faces, nothing goes right,
So much goes wrong.
Pressured to do things I don't want to do,
I wish for my happy childhood again.
But now I have to live whatever life throws at me,
The future awaits me.

Rhiannon Culley (12)
Holywells High School, Ipswich

The Time

The time controls the world
The time can stop the world
Time is unstoppable
Time is not controllable

If I could control the time
I would stop it when I please
I would pull jokes on people
And push them in the sea

I would travel back in time
I would make someone haunted
I would take back what is mine
I would make Daniel so he is wanted.

Ryan Shimmon (13)
Holywells High School, Ipswich

I Remember

I remember when you held my hand
and we played all night in the sand.
I remember when I bought ice cream
and it made me scream!
I remember when I fell on the floor
and I banged my head on the door.
I remember when I danced to my favourite song
and danced all night long.
I remember when my rabbit died
And I really, really cried.
I remember when I threw sand
and the other girl went mad!

Sydney Lawson-Whitear (12)
Holywells High School, Ipswich

The Gritty City

I am fire, I like to spread
Like butter on bread
You can run fast, but I'll always be ahead
When I am done I'll have a crown on my dangerous head
I like to destroy things in my path
Stay clear of my wrath
I clean a city like you in a bath
So build your craft and paddle real fast
Because this line is the last . . .

Jordan Cook & Brad Goodchild (13)
Holywells High School, Ipswich

The Most Beautiful Girl

She is the most beautiful girl in the world.
She smells as fragrant as a flower.
Her eyes are as blue as tropical lagoons.

She is a beautiful butterfly.
Our love is stronger than an ox.
She thrives elegance and beauty.

She lights up lives in a tick.
She is the sun to the sky.

Charlie Duric-Last (13)
Holywells High School, Ipswich

War

An empty village all alone,
Where lonely spirits moan and groan.
Once filled with happiness and singers,
Now only the cry of a child lingers.

This was caused by hate and war,
Dug into them right to the core.
Only the lucky few survive,
Rest died to stay alive.

Olivia Halsey (13)
Holywells High School, Ipswich

The One Who Made My Heart Shine

This is for the one who made my heart shine,
Who makes me get up in the bright morning.
The sole reason for the tears I cry,
He is why, from life, I keep on falling.

I'm like a sun fighting with an eclipse,
No matter how hard I try, he still wins.
When I see him, is when my stomach flips,
When he is around, my whole world spins.

Chloe Louise Bartrum (13)
Holywells High School, Ipswich

Parents

Parents say, 'Pack your bag for school.'
They sometimes make me look a fool!
They sometimes can be very useful,
And also can be very cool.
They can be very annoying,
but a lot of the time they're awesome,
Like, they take you cool places
And that's why they are the best!

Ben Aldous (12)
Holywells High School, Ipswich

Food Weather

There's weather outside
But it's all made of food.
'The snow is ice cream,' someone cried.
It made everyone in the mood.

Lemonade rain, sugar frost,
The world went insane, normal weather was lost.
'It's a food thunderstorm,' everyone said
While an eggy sun smiled overhead.

But then it gets much, much worse
A spaghetti twister comes first
Then giant meatballs, the size of a plane,
Oh my God, it's a food hurricane!

'My house is destroyed!' A tree fell down
'I'm so annoyed!' he began to frown.
Everyone began to run for their lives
But something took them by surprise.

The marshmallow clouds began to clear
The normal weather was back.
Everyone was stopping running in fear
No longer did we have a weather snack.

No longer did the people live in fear
Of food destroying their lives.
But there was a lot of mess left there
So everyone picked up their forks and knives

And ate!

Thomas Desborough (13)
Kemnal Technology College, Sidcup

World Cup Battle

Thirty-two teams have risen to the top
One by one they start to drop
Battling in groups to find the best
Winning is the ultimate test

Supporters wave their flags and cheer
They lift their glasses of golden beer
One by one the players appear
Knowing that the game is near.

The whistle blows, the ball is passed
Rooney runs and shows his class
Beats two players and aims for goal
The keeper is left in a hole.

One-nil up the whistle blows
They move on to fight another foe
This is the final, the decisive test
To sort out the best from the rest.

Jack Carnell (12)
Kemnal Technology College, Sidcup

The Saviour From Darkness

Screams fill the air
People running everywhere
Children know there is no care
Help! The apocalypse is here!

Monsters walk the dying land
People pray for God's hand.
Time slips away like sand
Help! The apocalypse is here!

Finally, from the surf
A hero comes to save the Earth.
Banishing the monsters from our turf
Once again peace flourishes.

Connor Tompsett (12)
Kemnal Technology College, Sidcup

What Am I?

I can make a world with a pencil
And sky with a song
The sea with string
And a cave as big as Hong Kong.

A sky with green stars
Can be made with a brush
An unusual life form
With paper and other stuff.

I can free time with a flash
And travel with a lens.
I can create calm emotions
Or make you feel tense.

I've given you clues
Do you know what I am?
It's easier than you think, I know you can.
I am an artist.

Miles Taylor (13)
Kemnal Technology College, Sidcup

Outer Space

Have you ever wondered what's up there high in outer space?
Astronauts flying everywhere finding nothing, it's a disgrace.
There could be a possibility that there is another race
Who are smart and more advanced and would laugh in our face.
They could be any shape or size, we will never know,
Maybe they're travelling here right now, it's just they're really slow.
But we should welcome them with our arms open wide
Or we could destroy them with our weapons and force them to hide.
This is the end of my poem; I hope you thought it was fun
And remember there could be aliens past the moon and past the sun.

Michael Beven (12)
Kemnal Technology College, Sidcup

Haiku Poems

The mountains are close,
The sun is shining on them,
It looks like the night.

The sun is shining,
The beach is full of people,
Summertime is here.

The wind is blowing,
I can't hear myself thinking,
It is cold today.

The sea waves are rough,
The waves crash against the wall,
I am getting wet.

I am playing games
Such as football and tennis,
They are very fun.

Harry Stapley (13)
Kemnal Technology College, Sidcup

What Is War?

A war is people with machinery and guns,
A lot of people losing loved ones.
They fight and fight all day, all night,
When soldiers die they walk into the light.
It causes depression and pain,
It will not end until everyone has been slain.
The end would spread happiness and relief,
Loss would cause a lot of grief.
War is a fight for land, power and money
So put a stop to it so it can be sunny.

Jozef Szkoda (13)
Kemnal Technology College, Sidcup

Liverpool FC

Danny Agger is so great
In defence like a wall of slate
Mascherano in defensive midfield
He is like a human shield
Aquilani and Gerrard passing the ball all over the park
They can pinpoint a pass in the dark
Maxi Rodriguez on the right
Gives the defenders a real fright
Fernando Torres with so much pace
Scoring goals, what an ace!

Max Turner Howard (13)
Kemnal Technology College, Sidcup

Why I Follow Thee?

You ask why I follow Lord Jesus?
Why I love Him the way I do?
When the world's turned away from His teachings
And the people who serve Him are few.

It's not the rewards I'm after
Or gifts that I hope to receive.
It's the Presence that calls for my love,
It's the Spirit I trust and believe.

The Lord doesn't shelter His faithful
Or spare them all suffering and pain.
Like everyone else I have that boundary
And walk through my share of rain.

Yet He gives me a plan and a purpose
And that joy only the Christians have known.
I never know what comes tomorrow,
But I do know I'm never alone.

I can never be that Father,
I can never be that Man.
I am working and growing just to be like Him,
This I promise 'cause He knows I can.

I am going to lie underneath His wing,
I am going to be safe and sound.
No weapon fashioned against me shall prosper
Because that person shall be found.

It's the love always there when you need it,
It's the words that redeem and inspire.
It's the longing to ever be with Him,
That burns in my heart like a fire.

So you ask why I love my Lord Jesus?
Well friend that's so easy to see.
But the one thing that fills me with wonder is
Why Jesus loves someone like me.

Aneghe Regina Onodjamue (13)
Leigh Technology College, Dartford

Water Through And Through

Like the sea I am blue
I don't know what to do
My life is hard
I try to move on
Forgive and forget
So I don't want to get stressed
My friends don't listen
To what I have to say
I feel everything I do is wrong
So I try to sing that song
The song that's full of joy
But instead I'm sitting there
And no one cares
I cry and cry and cry
I can't see through my eyes
Like the sea I am blue
Water through and through
I don't know what to do
So I be myself every day
There must be a way
Like the sea I am blue.

Natalie Smith (12)
Marston Vale Middle School, Stewartby

Life

Life is hard but I gotta live through it
Through the bad times and the good
I've been through them all
Some times are hard
Some times are easy
Sometimes I don't think I can live
But I keep on thinking of the fun I can have with life
But don't worry; I'm still the same girl I used to be.

Shannon Gibson (12)
Marston Vale Middle School, Stewartby

Bad News, Good News

The telly is blurring, the news is on
First it is war, the fighting and pain.
The bombs and men, some dead
Families insane from heartbroken love.

Next it is a crash, a fatal one
Someone dead, maybe a dead family
From a lorry driver on his mobile
Or by rowdy children on a bus.

Then it is a missing person
Disappeared at night or just coming home from school.
Kidnapped or killed by an idiot, a stupid fool that is
The master of making people grieve or weep.

Then it is happiness! The one happy thing
Someone has made it to 100 years old
Or people have come home from war, finally.
I sigh with relief
There is some good in the world.

Eleanor Dunn (12)
Marston Vale Middle School, Stewartby

Embarrassed By Yourself

You start to change but hardly realise
Then you start to want your first kiss and more.

This alarms you of what's happening
You cut yourself off from everyone else
Because you're too embarrassed.

You're too afraid to show and say
Because you think you're different.

Whereas I'm not afraid
As I'm not ashamed
Because I know I'm not different
As we all grow up.

Megan Rowe (12)
Marston Vale Middle School, Stewartby

We Have One Thing In Common

It's turning twelve and I'm hungry
But it's not just me
Every person may feel hungry in a day
But for some people it never goes away.
For people in Africa
This feeling never goes away
It's with them every step of the way
Every step,
Every day.

Hunger and thirst
Is not the feeling you will burst
It feels you have no power
No energy, no happiness.
But there is one thing
We have in common
The love we have for
Our family.

Emilia Bugg (12)
Marston Vale Middle School, Stewartby

You'll Get Through It

Life can be really hard at times
Like when you lose someone close
Or your parents' divorce.
You need to get over it though
And eventually you will.
All you need is someone friendly
To hug and comfort you.
Find a friend to get you through it
Or maybe a member of family.
So you will soon cheer up
Don't stay down in the dumps.
Just take my advice to help you
Through the hardest part of life.

Ellie Bancroft-Blake (12)
Marston Vale Middle School, Stewartby

All I Hear From You

The only words I hear from you are
'What am I meant to do?'
You expect me to tell you everything
And you don't even say thank you.

There are some things I find hard too you know
But still I hear the same words
'What am I meant to do?' they ask
It really is absurd.

When then I can't tell you
Because I don't understand
You shout and you moan at me
And make me feel bad.

Those are the only words I hear from you
You never bother to say anything else to me
Stop moaning and stop shouting
Let me be free, stop using me.

Alex Keech (12)
Marston Vale Middle School, Stewartby

Changes

Some people like to have a change
Some people find them strange
Changes are a part of life
They are a part of you.

Changes happen all around
Sometimes they are without a sound
Changes are a part of life
They are a part of you.

A lot of changes are bad
Some make people sad
Changes are a part of life
They are a part of you.

Abigail Perrin (12)
Marston Vale Middle School, Stewartby

Love And Life

Life, there's the beginning, the end and the part in the middle
Some people we meet also talk in riddles.
We have friends, enemies and pets we adore
Friendship can turn into something more.
Sit in amazement from thinking of life
Marriage vows for husband and wife.
The children we have is a cycle of nature
We all evolved from a small tiny creature.

The next topic I'm going to start
It's the massive emotion you feel with your heart.
You cannot help the feeling inside
The feeling of when two hearts collide
It is one emotion you cannot escape
But sometimes love can cause heartache.
Contentment, resentment are all parts of life
And emotions will prevail through trouble and strife.

Tia Harris (12)
Marston Vale Middle School, Stewartby

Some People

Some people are small
Some people are tall
Some people are quiet
Some people are loud
Some people are tanned
Some people are pale
Some people are strong
Some people are weak
Some people are popular
Some people are disliked
Some people are poor
Some people are rich
Everyone is different
And we have to accept them all.

Harriet Beacon (12)
Marston Vale Middle School, Stewartby

Rules

I agree with most rules that are enforced
But one day we will all choose a different course.
Not to be clones of each other
To be a bit different from one another.
To have a wide range of things we may wear
Not ripped off a personality that cannot bear.
To wear flowers and bows, is that a crime?
As it is our body and we are using our time
I care most about friends and personalities too
But I enjoy being named 'pretty' wouldn't you?
Without rules there would be danger walking our streets
But it's getting out of hand and causing me heat.
So I say to all teachers, let me be me
So that one day we may all be free!

Lucy Alexander (12)
Marston Vale Middle School, Stewartby

Friendship Is The Key

I was bullied when I was younger
It doesn't make me a pushover
It made me very self-conscious
I wish I told my friends.

One month has passed, it's still going on
It's getting worse and worse
I told my friends today, they made me feel myself again.

She came to me today, the bully
She tried to make me feel small again
She tried and tried, it didn't work
My friends stood up for me
Now I'm not self-conscious,
Friendship is the key.

Lauren Kirby (12)
Marston Vale Middle School, Stewartby

Life Is Hard

Life is hard
But we have to get through it.
People say that you have to get over it
But we just can't.
What happens when you lose someone?
You can lose your love,
You can lose your best friend,
But the worst of all is death.
I haven't lost anyone in my life yet
But I know someday I will,
I will feel pain
Life is hard!

Lowri Jones (12)
Marston Vale Middle School, Stewartby

They Say . . .

They say I hate your guts
They say you made me cry
They say you don't like me
They say go away
They say I want to be alone
They say don't talk to me
They say lots of gossip
They say so many things
Some are not all good but bad
What they say is not what matters
But what they feel is what counts.

Leah Carter (13)
Marston Vale Middle School, Stewartby

Together Forever

Our friendship is forever
We will always be together.
Knowing you is great
I am glad we are good mates.
You are always in my head
Whenever I go to bed.
We go to all the malls
And empty all the stalls.
I call you almost every night
As I see a beautiful sight.
Our friendship together forever.

Rianna Clark (12)
Marston Vale Middle School, Stewartby

Most People, But I . . .

Most people think books are lame,
But I . . . think they're amazing.
Most people think they have to look perfect,
But I . . . don't really care.
Most people want to be popular
But I'm . . . happy with the friends I've got.
Most people want more
But I'm . . . fine with less.
Most people think I'm weird because I read more than most people
But I'm . . . not most people, I'm just me!

Casey Page (13)
Marston Vale Middle School, Stewartby

Sometimes

Sometimes I find it difficult to say no.
Sometimes it's hard to give life a go.
Sometimes it's hard to show and tell
What I have hidden inside so well.
Sometimes it's hard to stand and speak aloud.
Sometimes it's hard to stay seated down.
Sometimes it's hard to face your fears
Because you think it'll end in tears
But if you don't try you'll never know
So you should always give life a go!

Rebecca Stanton (11)
Marston Vale Middle School, Stewartby

Life

Life is fun and full of joy
Life is exciting, I'm always overjoyed
Life is loving with my great family
Life is enjoyable with great adventures
Life is good fun with family and friends.

I am me and always will be
I love my life the way it is.

Megan Creamer (11)
Marston Vale Middle School, Stewartby

Don't Leave

'Don't leave, please Dad, I want you to stay.'
'I know but Mum doesn't want it this way.'
So he leaves with a kiss and gets in his car
I cry on the doorstep with Ben by my arm.
I run to his car to plead once more
But he drives away and I see him no more.

Holly Smith (12)
Marston Vale Middle School, Stewartby

Just Stop And Stare

The sun and the moon and the creatures that we see
Many colours, different sizes, don't you want to stop and see
The wonders of nature and tranquillity, the sea and the sky
What a beautiful sight to see.

Many people don't realise what we have in our hands
Is time for someone to make a stand
Before our world become a ruined and destroyed place
It's time to save our world, including the human race.

So come on, what are we waiting for, make a start today
Recycle, reuse and reduce today
It's time to make a historical change for life as we know it
May not be there one day.

Mohammed Ibrar Ali Razaq (13)
Putteridge High School, Luton

Ups And Downs

Tears are aching in my heart
Everywhere I go I feel unwanted, depressed, lost
With this dark atmosphere around me
Happiness comes at a cost.

I called at your house but no one was there
I looked in the park but there's no one to care
I feel so alone, I feel so left out
I want to feel better but I'm full of self doubt.

I went to the party and found all my friends
It wasn't so bad I suppose it depends
Things start to look better, my tears are now dry
I don't understand what is making me cry.

Tears were aching in my heart
Everywhere I went I felt unwanted, depressed, lost
The dark atmosphere has now lifted
Happiness is here, I feel gifted.

Alice Cole (12)
Ranelagh School, Bracknell

Seasons

Spring is when snow melts away
It's another year, hip, hip, hooray!
We get to plant some flowers.

The seasons always change our mood
Quite a bit, like eating nice food
Some are quite miserable
Others are fantastical.

Summer's when the sun comes out
And we all eat some ice cream
We all have fun in the garden.

The seasons always change our mood
Quite a bit, like eating nice food
Some are quite miserable
Others are fantastical.

Autumn's when the leaves fall out
And we all have to sweep
All the leaves in the garden.

The seasons always change our mood
Quite a bit, like eating nice food
Some are quite miserable
Others are fantastical.

Winter's when the snow comes out
And we all make snowmen
And we drink hot chocolate.

The seasons always change our mood
Quite a bit, like eating nice food
Some are quite miserable
Others are fantastical.

Robert Dyster (12)
Ranelagh School, Bracknell

Locked Inside Myself

I don't know what to do
My anger is building up
I can feel my blood pumping
I'm going to explode

Just want to tell someone
But know I cannot
Everything is annoying me
Building up

Should I tell
Or would I lash out?
Would it be worse?
Would I regret?

I want to do right but don't know how
Could they be right that I should tell?
But what would the bully do?
It might just get worse!

It happened to someone else once
She moved schools
I don't want to do that
My friends are all here.

Maybe I should stand up
And fight for myself
But if I did would it really help?
I don't know what to do!

I feel like the key has been locked
Like my voice cannot be heard
I can feel my blood pumping
I'm going to explode.

Rachel Lammin (13)
Ranelagh School, Bracknell

The Move

Today is the day of our move
Mum and Dad are stressed out
The cat's not about
My brother and I are starting to shout
It seemed so far away
But today is the day
Cos today we move out.

Today is the day of our move
In the kitchen of clutter
'Mum, where's the butter?'
Everyone's all mutter, mutter, mutter
Tempers are frayed
No time to delay
Cos today we move out.

Today's the day of our more
Strange men packing my stuff
If that's not enough
They've even taken the loo brush
Mum says I should pack
But the removal man, Bill and Mack
Have already taken half my room
Cos today we move out.
Today's the day of our move
As we get in the car
With tears in our eyes
Not knowing what new adventures we seek
It's been a long way there
But we have finally done it
Cos today we move in.

Madeleine Oliver (12)
Ranelagh School, Bracknell

A Life Of An Eagle

Through eagle's eyes I view below
Mountain tops with coats of snow.

In seas of blue, the creatures glide
Seeking hollows where they hide.

Deserts dry all parched from heat
Has hidden life to dart and streak.

Waterfalls and white bleached sand
Endless wonders all fill this land.

Rivers twist and pavement roams
Carry travellers far from homes.

Meadows sweet of buds and grass
Welcome refuge from life so fast.

Lightning torches trees so tall
Tornado and hurricanes make cities fall.

Torrential rains and floods that bash
Nature's way to take out our trash.

Man may wonder how to command
Bounty of places that cover this land.

But to the eagles who fly way up high
All are God's gifts free for the eyes.

Adam Chave-Jones (12)
Ranelagh School, Bracknell

Happiness

Happiness is when you smile at me.
Happiness is knowing you are a friend to me.
Happiness is smiling about the secrets we share.
Happiness is knowing that you are there.
Happiness is easy when you're around,
A special friend in you I've found.
Good times, laughter, sharing this friendship forever after.

Amy Butcher (12)
Ranelagh School, Bracknell

A Place To Be

A place is a place
A place to be
A place to share
With you and me.

A racing track is a place
A place to be
A place with cars
Going far.

New York is a place
A place to be
A place with shops
Until you drop.

Hawaii is a place
A place to be
A place with fruits
As exotic as can be.

A place is a place
A place to be
A place to share
With you and me.

Georgina Wood (12)
Ranelagh School, Bracknell

Chocolate

Dark chocolate, white chocolate
Chocolate is so yummy
Milk chocolate, nutty chocolate
Chocolate in my tummy.

Chocolate in your mouth
Melting on your tongue
Chocolate on your teeth
Make your snack last long!

Luke Seymour (12)
Ranelagh School, Bracknell

Jobs

I want to be an artist
Just like Van Gogh
Painting lovely pictures
Chopping my ear off

I want to be Prime Minister
Deciding important things
Running the country
And meeting queens and kings

I want to own a sweetie shop
Selling something sweet
Buying lots of chocolate bars
And lovely things to eat

I want to be an archaeologist
Digging in the dirt
And if I fall into a tomb
I hope I don't get hurt

I don't want to be a teacher
I'd waste my life away
Teaching naughty children
On minimum pay.

Maisie Turner (12)
Ranelagh School, Bracknell

The Sea

I watch the sea and the sea watches me
It splashes over my hands and feet
The chill of it washes through me
Although soon after warmth takes the seat
The gulls sweep low when the tide is out
Though watch when they fly when they turn about
The sea is strong it has no end
Few go out and return again.

Emily Wilson (12)
Ranelagh School, Bracknell

The Crash

The pain tears through me
Like a thousand knives
If I'd stuck to the rules
It wouldn't have cost them their lives.

I was on top of the world
I'd thought for a minute
But I should have been sensible
And stuck to the limit.

Whizzing round the corners
Like I was king of the hill
Not even realising
Who I was about to kill.

Innocent people
Who had committed no crime
I wish it had been me
Who was killed at the time.

The pain tears through me
Like a thousand knives
If I'd stuck to the rules
It wouldn't have cost them their lives.

Sophie Adams (12)
Ranelagh School, Bracknell

Saturn

Saturn twists and turns with light
Saturn rings are so bright
Saturn has sixteen moons
Saturn's fans are all loons
Saturn is made of gas
Saturn has a very big mass
Saturn has very big rings
Saturn has some other things.

Catherine Powell (12)
Ranelagh School, Bracknell

When I Rule The World

When I rule the world
I'll hand out free food
Clean water as well
Everyone I will include
'It's free!' I yell.

When I rule the world
The young will join the old
Have fun together
In rain or heat or cold
No matter what the weather.

When I rule the world
The poor will have good jobs
The homeless all have homes
They'll be no more need for mobs
Or fights or mobile phones.

When I rule the world
I'm so excited for that day
We will learn to love each other
As we work and rest and play
When I rule the world.

Naomi Koefman (12)
Ranelagh School, Bracknell

What We Need

There's always a rainbow when it's raining
And the sun is shining too
But sometimes there's no hope
For me and you.

We need to shout out loud from the rooftops
We want peace.
We've got to show the whole world somehow
What we need
We need, peace, peace and not peas!

Alice Harvey (12)
Ranelagh School, Bracknell

Hammy

Once upon a time I have a hamster
And Hammy was his name.
He lived in a wooden cage
And ate seeds and nuts all day.
Chip, our border collie
Loved to sit and watch him play
He was motionless for hours
And did the same every day.

Hammy wanted a girlfriend
He dreamt about one every day
With fluffy golden yellow fur
And sparkling dark blue eyes.
But Hammy's very fussy
And all the girls we tried
Completely turned their backs on him
And he poked them in the eye!

So Hammy will stay lonely
As a partner we can't find
Until a lonely lady hamster
Makes him change his mind.

Emma Sidey (11)
Ranelagh School, Bracknell

My Lyrical Poem

Rugby, rugby,
How I love rugby.
You can tackle and duck
And make for the ruck.
We score a try to make the opponents cry.
They all say they have no luck.
I kick the ball but then I fall.
I take him out without a doubt,
We win the game to put them to shame,
All for the fame.

Blake Wilson (12)
Ranelagh School, Bracknell

Why Can't I Think Of Anything To Write?

Why can't I think of anything to write
It should be easy, shouldn't it?
There's hundreds of thousands of subjects out there
And I can't think of one.

There's bullying and polar bears
The Victorians and the world
Shopping centres, my school,
Toys and friends

Or different styles of poems
Acoustic and rhyming are just some.

Maybe a haiku
A simple poem to write
But it's very short.

Why can't I think of anything to write
It should be easy, shouldn't it?
There's hundreds of thousands of subjects out there
And I can't think of one!

Eleanor Nicolaides (12)
Ranelagh School, Bracknell

Mystery Object

The rusted red bonnet has a slight sheen to it in the sunlight
Green mould infests the steering wheel making it horrible to touch
The black seat is forever wet, a home for the excess rainwater
But the engine runs bold and strong
A lion in a ramshackle cage, (despite needing a jump start)

From the rear end spray fragments of what it has chopped down
Finding their way into every nook and every cranny
The levers are stiffer that a bike with no oil
Though once going they work in full agreement with each other
With a cough and a splutter these parts come to form . . .

My lawnmower.

Will Norman (12)
Ranelagh School, Bracknell

Magic Swing

The old swing sitting there
Creaky, wooden, rusty, square.
No one loves it, no one cares
About the old swing sitting there.

Daily and nightly it was used
Bright, blue, fun and new.
A girl with plaits sat upon it
Hopes and dreams wished within it.

As summers come and summers go,
The swings used less as the child grows.
Hopes and dreams are now granted
In the old swing they were planted.

The old swing sitting there
Creaky, wooden, rusty, square.
No one loves it, no one cares
But does anyone know
What magic lived there?

Beth Carpenter (12)
Ranelagh School, Bracknell

The Avocado

Avocado, mainly green,
Very sweet, not normally mean.
It has a stone
Of dark brown tone.
Cut it in half and scrape it out
If you listen, you'll hear a shout.
'Don't eat my guts, please eat the pear
I am bald, whereas he has hair.'
But the avocado is the best
In salads or alone, it beats the rest!

James Cunningham (12)
Ranelagh School, Bracknell

Friendship

You will know when you are friends with me
Because we'll always be together
Through good times and bad times
Our friendship will last forever.

You and me are friends forever
It's like our own little Heaven
No one can ever split us up
We are friends 24/7.

And if you ever go away
And we're so far apart
You just remember this
You're always in my heart.

Chloe Giles (12)
Ranelagh School, Bracknell

Just On Your Own

Guitar, guitar you are a star
With a tune and a song that we can sing along
If you played with the drums
There'd be more noise to come.

Guitar, guitar you are a star
If you played with a voice
It'd be a little high-pitched
So play with a trumpet to save you from the ditch.

Guitar, guitar you are a star
To play on your own is rather very mean
But guitar, guitar you sound best alone with you and your strings
Just on your own!

Frankie Overton Hatton (12)
Ranelagh School, Bracknell

Snow

Dainty snowflakes
Drifting slowly to the ground
Settling there
To form a beautiful blanket.

Children running outside
Ready to make the first snow footprints
Wrapped up in warm clothes
They walk through the winter wonderland.

Melting snow
Drips that were once icicles roll down the windows
The water that was once snow is absorbed by the ground.
Silence falls.

Katie Scott (12)
Ranelagh School, Bracknell

Four Seasons

Sparkling spring, lambs all play
Sparkling spring, new life each day.

Summer sunshine, the sky is blue
Summer sunshine to share with you.

Amazing autumn the colours bright
Amazing autumn, artists delight.

Windy winter, the snowflakes fall
Windy winter, shivering all!

Molly Greenfield (12)
Ranelagh School, Bracknell

The Chair

The chair sat unwanted in the pouring rain
Nobody cared for its suffering and pain.
They all came outside when the weather was hot
Though it sat all alone when the sun was not.
As the rain soaked through its wooden seat
No one's heart would miss a beat.
They only noticed when the moon was long gone,
The chair was broken, forgotten and forlorn.

Olivia Winter (12)
Ranelagh School, Bracknell

I Must Survive

The rain is beating, torturing, soaking, drenching, I must survive.
I'm running quickly, escaping, hopefully, I must survive.
The beast is following, pursuing, scaring, snarling, I must survive.
I'm turning, splashing, speeding, almost crashing, I must survive.
Suddenly I'm tripping, falling, tumbling downwards, I must survive.
I'm nearly there, hurrying, scurrying, fast as I can, I must survive.
Then I'm through the door, crashing, bashing onto the floor.
Somehow I survived.

Eden Sinclair (11)
Ranelagh School, Bracknell

War

Flying mortars crunching through the sky
Like birds of prey seeking their source of life . . .
But bringing death.
Relentless, searing heat sapping energy.
Enemies, hundreds fall day by day.
Isolated, bare necessities gone.
We still fight on
Making us hungry to kill.

Josh Brown (11)
Ranelagh School, Bracknell

Hate

This is a poem about hate, the thing that boils up inside you
A volcano of boiling animosity, secretly you tremble at its power.

Hate follows you everywhere, you turn around and it's there.
Hate seeks you out, entering your life, destroying your life.
Hate takes over your mind and soul and we are left helpless in its wake.

Euan Farrow (12)
Ranelagh School, Bracknell

Winter To Spring

Everyone is happy, winter's almost done
No one wants to see snow again, even though it's fun
Now that spring is on its way the flowers show their faces
And children rush out to play to join in all the races.
The world feels so much better now the days are getting lighter
All those sad winter moods are feeling so much brighter.

James Moul (12)
Ranelagh School, Bracknell

Smiling

Smiling is infectious; you can catch it like the fly
If I blew the smile it would land on you.
When I was walking people saw my feature
But this feature was caught as if they were a creature.
I thought about this giant smile and realised how much it's worth
A smile just as big as this could travel round the Earth!

Jack Leyland (12)
Ranelagh School, Bracknell

The Yuki Within Me

Upon a hill, our old favourite den,
I stand and gaze at the swirling sky.
Watching the flurry of white falling snow,
I remember you,
And all the good memories we share.

Two babies coiled together inside their mother's womb,
And then down from the sky it floated to greet us to the world,
The snow.
It became your namesake, you having been the first into the light,
Yuki.

Two children playing together in the white soft snow,
Laughing, giggling and enjoying each other's company.
You were so similar to your namesake,
Pure, fun and delicate, you attracted friendship and were my
best friend,
My Yuki.

Two adolescents standing together in the snow,
One protecting the other against the loathing of peers.
Still I could compare you to snow,
A strong force and protective if needed, yet soft and gentle when
caring for me,
Yuki, your promise of love for me was unconditional.

Two young adults trapped together in a storm,
Cold, white, angry snow, a great unstoppable force,
Just like you when you faced those who hated the true me.
But then it took you, the gentle cold snow,
And I gripped you close in the blanket of snow, Yuki, and wept.

One adult standing alone at an old place of memories,
Staring at the flurry of white snow I remember you,
And how you always loved and protected me even when others
turned away.
No other guy could ever take your place inside my heart,

My Yuki, live on, inside me.

Jessica Campbell (17)
Sandhurst School, Sandhurst

Traveller

I am not what I wish to be.
I am not happy as I am.
I am the product of my life which is not as I wish it to be.
I have the power to change, yet I hesitate.

Why do you hesitate?

I wish I knew.
I have seen many things in my short existence.
I will continue to exist for the ages,
I am not happy as I am.

How do you wish you were?

I wish I was a traveller.
I want to flee, to run . . . to fly.
I want to fly from my problems, for they cannot follow.
I want to leave and travel.

Travel where?

I wish to travel the stars, the worlds and the edge.
I am to travel the length and depth of creation.
I will see eternity and be at peace.
I will become eternal.

How will this occur?

My mind will wander.
My soul will ravel.
My body will remain.
I will have become the traveller.

Jack Day (16)
Sandhurst School, Sandhurst

Night-Time Museum

Have you ever wondered
What goes on
In museums
At night?

The doors close
The locks click
I turn around
And guess what I see?

In the museums
All the animals live
The stone statues
Start to walk.

Nothing is clear
Until next morn
They all go back
All so innocent.

But I know
What I saw
In the museum
At night.

Emma-Louise Downe (13)
Sandhurst School, Sandhurst

Olimpia - My Little Delight

My hamster is tiny and cute,
she would fit in a newborn baby's boot.
She has four little paws
and lots of tiny claws.
She squeaks and eats
and then runs in her wheel
Olimpia - my little delight.

Bryony Ford (12)
Sandhurst School, Sandhurst

Autumn Fun

Gorgeous colours on the trees
The rock hard ground covered in leaves.
Mini hedgehogs here and there
Hear the distant music from the fair
Crimsons, golds and oranges too
Browns, black but no gracious blues.
Having fun with my silly friends
I wish the autumn would never end.
Autumn fun is so great
Love the autumn, hope it's not late.
Bonfires, Halloween, my birthday too
Love the sound of the autumn tunes.

Megan Humphrey (12)
Sandhurst School, Sandhurst

Beach

Your first steps on the warm summer's day, the sand as soft as a silk blanket
A light breeze smoothing your arms, the smell of seafood and chocolate ice cream
The sound of children splashing the glazed calm sea, the taste of sandy sandwiches tickle your tastebuds.
As you lay on the warm soft towel the sea calls you inviting you to come,
As you walk forward your feet begin to sink in the now damp wet sand.
You walk in, the sea so breathtaking as warm as a bath.
You look up at the sky, the sun burning your nose
While surrounded by a deep blue blanket fish swim by every colour and shade.
As you admire their beauty you close your eyes and appreciate the burning hot sun
Hearing only muffled voices from the world around you.
Not bothering to open your eyes, relaxed as if you were in a trance.

Aimée Mundy (13)
Southend High School for Girls, Southend-on-Sea

The Status Quo

They think that she's strange
They think that she's different
And they think that she's weak and alone
But really it's them who are weak.

So she hears their whispers
Grow louder each day
Until she cannot ignore them anymore
So she pretends for them.

She laughs at the new girl
She says that she's strange
And everyone sniggers but her
So with a tear in her eye, she watches her sit alone and afraid.

So they all grow up
With jobs that they hate
And they wished they'd worked hard at school
They wished they'd been like that girl who was different and strange.

She grew up too
And much like the rest
She couldn't even remember the names
Of the people for whom she had changed.

Another life lost
To the status quo
Another mould unbroken
Another unhappy soul.

Nancy Jones (13)
Southend High School for Girls, Southend-on-Sea

Nothing

Once or twice in a lifetime
A strange thing occurs
Maybe a donkey sucking on a lime
Or a nerd eating a bird.

I woke up on a Friday
As depressed as you could be
All I wanted to do was to lay
And think of the Indian sea.

But still I stepped out of bed
And stepped out the door
Not ready for another day of Fred
Not sure if I could handle anymore.

Instead of walking down my stairs
I saw a set of stones
On the walls were pictures of bears
As well as a pile of bones.

As I wandered under
This deep and dark cave
I heard the sound of thunder
As striking as the grave.

I suddenly got scared
Thinking I was lost
If anyone actually cared
What about my boss?

My boss wouldn't be content
But I couldn't think of that
The tunnel had got almost bent
I could have sworn I saw a bat.

Suddenly I heard a noise
Thumping footsteps on the floor
I was hoping they weren't alive toys
I've had enough stress and don't want more.

I heard a large roar
And looked to see
A large fleshless boar

Fly right over me.

Then I saw a man run right in front of me
Holding a tin can, he told me to hold onto it
He clicked his fingers, I heard the sea.
I wasn't sure what was happening to me.

When I opened my eyes
I was back at home
What a surprise
But I was only on my own!

Jessica Allen (12)
Southend High School for Girls, Southend-on-Sea

Turkey

The doors of the outside air open and *whoosh* a gush of suffocating warmth hits you
It takes your breath away, the searing sun beaming down on you
Momentarily you're blinded from the brightness, the exotic smell of the Turkish air revives you
You watch the people in the swimming pools, splashing and splishing, laughing and larking
The beautiful proud palm trees stand tall
The scene of freshly mowed grass and exotic colourful flowers excites you
As you carry on walking you watch the sunbathers lying motionless
Absorbing the searing sunlight and listening to the birds tweet and twitter with joy.
Then you stop and stand still like a frozen statue.
You're there staring at the white sand and the Mediterranean Sea
Listening to the loud cheerful waves with the bright scorching sun shining down on you
You're at the beach at last, it's paradise,
You can't help just running, feeling the hot burning sand between your toes.
Running as fast as you can, like you're being chased
Then leap into the inviting sea feeling the cool salty water engulf you.

Ayda Khanchi (13)
Southend High School for Girls, Southend-on-Sea

Angels Are Taking You

Alone we lay
Staring into the night sky.
We have nothing to say
I lay there and think why
The angels are taking you.

I look deep into your eyes
I'm the first to look away
You hold my cheek, I cry,
It's cos I know you are not to stay

The angels are taking you.
You grab my hand
I hold you real tight,
You tell me to be strong
And that we have the whole night
Although the angels are taking you.

I close my tear-filled eyes
And remember all the memories.
All the good times
The ones with you and me
The angels are taking you.

All the times we went to the park
Or you came round mine
The times you made me really laugh
We had some real good times
The angels are taking you.
When we found out
We weren't quick enough
The cancer had spread too much
Though it didn't stop our love
The angels are taking you.

You kiss me
And whisper, 'I love you.'
You close your eyes
And your last breath you drew.
The angels are taking you.

I cried, 'I love you too.'
You smiled at me Will
Will, you're now lifeless
Your body lay still
The angels have taken you.

Rachele Anne Lewis (13)
Southend High School for Girls, Southend-on-Sea

The Noise

Silence.
There's nobody there,
Darkness, darkness everywhere,
Silence.

Where am I to go?
I cannot see, I do not know,
Silence.

Wait, what's that noise?
The noise, can you hear it?
Tap tappity tap, tap tappity tap

Listen, it's getting closer
It's coming from that door
Tap tappity tap, tap tappity tap

Let's open it
Come on,
Tap tappity tap, tap tappity tap

Ssh, stop barking
You'll let it know we're here
Tap tappity tap, tap tappity tap

Now let's open the door
On no, it's too stiff, push push
Tap tappity tap, tap tappity tap . . .

Oh phew, it's open
But what's that over . . . ?
Silence.

Laura Felton-Hustwitt (13)
Southend High School for Girls, Southend-on-Sea

The Sales

My favourite mall
Far too small
Not enough room
The changing rooms loom.

Tight mini-skirt
I'm better off with a shirt
Light summer dress
Enough with the stress
Far too small
Return to the stall.

Bigger size
The tags
Small, priced lies
Return to the rooms
The ones that loom.

Try it on
Try not to rip
Over my head
Oh look, there's the zip!

Up to the queue
Might nip in a snooze
What have I got to lose?

Paid at the till
Lots of money still
At my favourite mall.

Abigail Kelly (13)
Southend High School for Girls, Southend-on-Sea

Ashfield

As I walked down the tiny lane
Of the small village called Ashfield
I looked up in the pitch-black sky to see
A thousand stars look down on me.

The wind brushed softly past my ears
Everything was as quiet as a mouse
Just my footsteps leading me on
Where was I going?

Finally I'm here on the main road
There a car goes flying past
I can taste the dampness on my tongue
I can taste the smoke of the fire in the field.

I take a deep breath in
The fresh air hits my nostrils
It's all so sweet and sticky
On this late and lonely lush night.

I walk closer to the field
Like a tiger edging towards its prey
The stubbly silk of the horse's head
Brushes against my shoulder.

My grandma and grandad's house is in sight
Only a few more paces to go
I look up as the clouds mask the starry night
I anticipate the rain is coming.

Isabella Wolfe (13)
Southend High School for Girls, Southend-on-Sea

It Was All A Dream

Midnight struck, I was stuck inside
No one was there to see
I ran through the corridors looking everywhere
Searching frantically.

I was shaking and scared and all I could hear
Were noises down the hall
As shadows began to emerge
From their hiding place behind the wall.

I reached the door but it was locked
I was stuck here for the night
From behind me I heard a noise
I screamed and turned in fright.

There before me stood a beast
With teeth as large as chairs
I ran but I had nowhere to go
So I made a break for it up the stairs.

The beast followed me and
Just as he grabbed my arm
I woke up in my bed
Everything was calm.

It was just a dream, that's all it was
But how can I be sure?
I pinched my skin just to see and it became clear
The beast was no more.

Annabelle Abrahams (12)
Southend High School for Girls, Southend-on-Sea

Summer

The summer air, so warm and fresh
The grass so green and the sky so blue
Daisies all around, scattered in the field
The warming smell of pollen fills my nose.

Laying on the beach, soaking up the sun
With the calming sea breeze brushing my hair
The sound of whooshing waves
As smooth as a sheet of silk.

Ice creams and lollipops and a chill through my body
Slowly cooling me down
The sound of children's laughter fills the air
The hot and radiant sun beating down.

The colourful butterflies dance around
As light as feathers and as graceful as ballet dancers
Cooking barbeques fill me with hunger
Like a lion ready to pounce on its prey.

I take a dip in the glistening pool
And swim and glide like a dolphin
I sunbathe some more
And then take a walk on the light and fluffy sandy beach.

Oh how I love summer
The air so warm and so fresh.

Jessie Stack (13)
Southend High School for Girls, Southend-on-Sea

Vampire

The force of death necessary
The urge to kill was heeded
The desire to drain a body of blood was high
The pain to walk away was hard
But giving in felt worse
Vampire.

Alya Omar (12)
Southend High School for Girls, Southend-on-Sea

Dominican Republic

A happy place
Wild and free
In my favourite place this is what I see.

The smell of fresh air
Caribbean island breeze
Hot stuffy air around me.

Sun is shining on my face
Shopping in my favourite place.

The taste of the jungle
And exotic fruits
Makes my mouth go crazy.

Birds chirping
Trees waving at me
Calling in my ear
These are things I hear.

Touching the beautiful sand
Letting it fall from my hand
Rubbing sun cream
Licking my lolly

Now I know I'm here
Welcome to the Dominican Republic.

Millie Guy (13)
Southend High School for Girls, Southend-on-Sea

My Pencil Case

When I come to school
My pencil case comes to life
It shivers and jumps
When it awakes from its deep sleep.

It changes colour
To suit its mood
And sometimes
It can be rather rude!

Yellow is happy
Bouncing with joy
Blue is upsetting
All low and destroyed.

Green is a dream
All alone in a cloud
And red is rage
Being so loud.

So, as you can see
My pencil case is
As bright as can be
And so happy and free!

Paloma Sanz (13)
Southend High School for Girls, Southend-on-Sea

Thorpeness

Fields of green litter the earth around me
Wilting bark gnarled and twisted
Safe and enclosing
Skies unfolding like a piece of paper
Salty air engulfs me in its sweet embrace
Each grain of sand intertwined
Locked into each other
Washing over me as smooth as silk
Skimming stones across slapping seas.

Lydia Prior (12)
Southend High School for Girls, Southend-on-Sea

City Of My Heart

A city once so perfect
Now full of hate and neglect.
A big crash moved the ground
Ash and smoke growling all around.

Buildings smashed down
No stopping now
Cars flew up in the air
Panic was everywhere.

Planes collided with the ground
Big noises filled the surrounding
Glass shattered near me
Creating a rough sharp sea.

I could see it in people's eyes
The look of shock and surprise
The day you left me caused
The earthquake in the city of my heart.

Meredith Mills (13)
Southend High School for Girls, Southend-on-Sea

Mist

There was a deep fog blanketing the sky
My whole street covered by one big lie.
An eerie silence filled the air
Thickening over time.

I looked into the misty surroundings
Faint outlines of objects in the distance
A pall filling all the blemishes that are usually exposed.

I hoped I would find my way through the mist
I wondered if I should turn back
I stood there in the chilling darkness . . .

Laura Bettany (13)
Southend High School for Girls, Southend-on-Sea

New York City

There are yellow taxis everywhere
It is as loud as a screaming baby
When I look up I see tall buildings
There are so many places to go!

You can go sight-seeing
You can shop until you drop
I ease along from block to block
Stopping to go into every shop.

It's full of diversity
Excitement and adversity
Visit the Statue of Liberty
Eat pizza in Little Italy.

You may have already guessed
That the most populous city in the states
Is New York City
Definitely my favourite place.

Jemima Bouch (12)
Southend High School for Girls, Southend-on-Sea

Easter

Easter is my favourite season,
Easter eggs are the reason.
Chocolate is my favourite food,
It puts me in a very good mood.
Hot cross buns taste yummy toasted,
Easter cards can be posted.
Lambs and chicks, the Easter bunny
Are very sweet and very funny.
But God is who I think of really
With my family whom I treasure dearly.

Katie Webster (13)
Southend High School for Girls, Southend-on-Sea

One Cold, Icy Winter

One cold, icy winter
A black cloud appeared
When my best friend decided
The finish was near.

She said I was useless
She said I was dumb
I didn't understand
My heart had gone numb.

That night I cried
This feeling is rare.
Goodbye my blue skies
Hello, my nightmares.

And now a summer sun
Is glistening on the pond
The dark clouds are done
But the dreams still go on.

Emily Muggleton (13)
Southend High School for Girls, Southend-on-Sea

The Darkness

I fear it so much when night-time comes, it seems to follow me.
It scares me even to think of it, a place where nothing can see me.
My eyes are open wide and my heart, beating fast, it really does haunt me.
I pray for light, morning light but is anyone listening to me?
Then I feel a slight heaviness on my eyes, what could this be?
I turn on my bed, rest my head and drift to a world beyond me . . .
Where the darkness starts again on me . . .

Eunice Christine Otoo (13)
Southend High School for Girls, Southend-on-Sea

Dream Within A Dream

I hope you find what you're looking for
And get where you're wanting to go.
For this reason here is why you left
But why I just don't know.

This big black cloud above my world
Rains more and more each day.
And the hole that burns inside my heart
Feels like it's here to stay.

The walls around that built my life
Are crashing down like waves.
That flow across the ocean's shore
For comfort, my heart craves.

But nothing lasts forever, I know
And time must carry on.
An endless vortex of shadowed dreams
That lead me to where I belong.

Amy Layzell (13)
Southend High School for Girls, Southend-on-Sea

Sadness

A tear rolling down her face
As she waved goodbye
Blinking to wash them out
The sadness inside.

A lump is stuck in her throat
As they drove afar
Swallowing it away
The sadness inside.

She starts shaking and turns faint
Feeling overwhelmed
Sits down to steady herself
The sadness inside.

Then she felt lost and alone
The pain hurt too much
It drove her to the end
The sadness inside.

Anna Price (11)
Southend High School for Girls, Southend-on-Sea

My Best Friend

The person that holds your hand when you're scared.
The person that commits to any of your dares.

The person whose texts wake you up in the morning.
The person who stops French lessons being boring.

The person who is your shoulder to cry on.
The person who you know you can rely on.

The person who turns up to all of your parties.
The person who eats all the blue Smarties.

The person you give the plumpest pillow.
The person who calls you her marshmallow.

The person who gives you fashion advice.
The person who laughs at your fear of mice.

The person you will stay with till the end.
The person you call your best friend.

Ruby Yeomans (13)
Southend High School for Girls, Southend-on-Sea

My First Love

The way his hazel eyes glisten.
The way his voice makes me step back and listen.
The way he shows his perfect white teeth.
The way this brings me a sigh of relief.
The way he is polite and calls me ma'am.
The way this reminds me that I am still a lamb.
The way he is my winning goal.
The way I know I am still a foal.
The way he is clean and eats his grub.
The way he makes me feel like a small cub.
The way he makes me shy and sick.
The way I know I am only a chick.
The way he swayed his bright blonde hair.
The way I know that life's not fair.
The way that he looked and smiled.
This can't be love, I'm only a child.

Hannah Jones (13)
Southend High School for Girls, Southend-on-Sea

Summer

It's always summer in the beautiful beaches of Jeddah.
The picturesque views of the landscape bring great excitement to me.
The serene sky, nearly as silent night, with only the joyful twittering of birds as sweet as honey.
The sizzling sun is a hot furnace warming up the happy holidaymakers.
As I lower my gaze, I realise the sky is only the beginning of a beautiful scenery.
The proud palm trees stand firmly forming a canopy with their immense leaves.
The soft sand tickles my feet feeling as smooth as silk.
The twinkling sea is as glazed as the surface of milk.
As the sun sinks the warmth decreases causing small ripples in the stunning sea.
It's always summer in the beautiful beaches of Jeddah.

Maariya Arshad (13)
Southend High School for Girls, Southend-on-Sea

The Road Of The Future

There is a road that goes past my house
The road of the future.
I take this road to see later life and
When my friends come round
They don't believe me
So I reply
With tears in my eyes,
'Don't judge my journey before you have walked my road.'
For those who believe
I know they are the friends for me.
One day
I will take them down this road
For them to know the later me.

Jasmine Tuson (12)
The Emmbrook School, Wokingham

Pollution

Once upon a time
When the world was full of magic.
Once upon a time
When your dreams will last forever
The grass was green,
The birds would sing
But no that wasn't enough.
The sun would shine
And you could see the stars
But still not enough.
Plumes of smoke,
The birds don't sing
And you can't see the stars.
If that's not enough
And you can't realise
You're ruining the Earth
Your Earth
My Earth
Our Earth.
It's going, we're losing it,
It's all your fault.
There's no beauty left
Just please stop!

Kerys Meredew (12)
The Emmbrook School, Wokingham

Just

It's just a tree
That stands in the field.
It's just a chair
Sitting all alone.
It's just a kite
Attached to a string.
It's just a stream
In the forest
And it's just the sky
There all the time.
But the tree is really a person
Dancing and singing for us all.
The chair is really your friend
Waiting for you whenever it's needed.
The kite is really a bird
Trying to break away and start its life.
The stream is really a horse
Exploring the world we never see
And the sky is really our home
There for when we need a break.

Chloe Moore (13)
The Emmbrook School, Wokingham

Rainforest

Oh rainforest was ever so green
All we have to do is keep clean.
Monkeys cheerfully playing
Side to side swaying.
Tigers prowling
While wolves are howling.
Bright coloured parrots
Watching bunnies eat carrots
As rain pours down
Still the animals don't frown.
What a lovely habitat
Although people try to kill with a bat.

So why be mean
Would you like that to happen to you?
So keep it green.
Someday go and see that wonderful scene
As well as happy chimpanzees.

Jordan Onraet-Wells (13)
The Emmbrook School, Wokingham

Is Death The Only Answer

Shell on frantic shell hammered on top
Yet our stuttered breaths still whimpered, non-stop,
The shrieking air, our choking gasps,
This unrelenting hell will never pass.
Rain, shells, blood guttering down,
The wrenching stench,
The awful loathsome sounds.

Our dire wounds, huge-bulged like squids,
God we pleaded, this malevolence, forbid,
Constantly enveloped in the mud, deluging muck,
The uninterrupted monotony, in time we are stuck.
The spewing of blood, no more tonight!
So I entered the dark, where I found the light.

William Parker (14)
The Leys School, Cambridge

What About Me?

For every basin filled
A little heart will die.
For you have gushing water
But no one hears my cry.

In the smoking hot sun
That burns through our skin.
You prepare delicious food
While I'll scavenge the bin.

Throbbing in my ear
My heart is racing fast.
You are putting your feet up
How long will it last?

My weak skeleton of a body
Struggles under the force.
You've seen the lurid adverts
Will nature take its course?

I'm over here
And you are over there.
Please! Will someone help me?
I have no time to spare.

Nicole Montague (13)
The Leys School, Cambridge

Their Name Liveth For Evermore

Normal youths
Just like us
Were forced to comply
With never a fuss.

'Seventh Hell,'
That's what we say
As we sit prostrate
Every day.

I sit helpless
My best friends' moans
Whilst my only injury
A few bruised bones.

Now thousands of
Machine guns splutter
Whilst sons and daughters
All mutter,

'What is happening?'
One child cried
'Is my father going to die?'
These children know
What none will admit
Not many will come home
Fighting fit.

Myself included
We started as twenty-five
Now under half have survived.
The cause of this?
Who really cares?
It's agony and suffering
That we men bear.

We rest in trenches
Through the night
The siren sounds
Now put out the light.

By now

We were familiar
With this dreadful noise
As were all
Sweet girls and boys.

It's what came next
That makes us afraid
Frantic shells hammer
Above where we lay.

I'm never coming back
To this awful post
Although I'm not the one
Who has suffered most.

As I live on
And continue to strive
Families wonder is this a worthy way
To end my son's life?

Harriet Prior (13)
The Leys School, Cambridge

No One Cared

Dark, too dark. Machine guns spluttered all around.
The trench which protected was my only hope now.
All the men knew why, they all knew who, but how,
How could anyone be truly inhumane,
To put a grown man through torture and pain?
'Gas! Gas! Put on your masks boys. Get your masks now!'
I can't find it! I can't find it! Where's my damn . . .'
A flicker of light passed over my closed eyes
Awoke to the painful noise of painful cries.
No longer in that dull, dark and dingy trench
Now alone sitting on the sunny park bench.
A few men stopped and stared and damned me a coward
Even the eyes of my fellows had glowered.

Alexandra Gray (14)
The Leys School, Cambridge

No Man's Land

The mist it's strong and no one sees
What dangers lie in no-man's-land
The guns are blazing across the land
Everywhere apart from no man's land.

The soldiers charge on the sound
That echoes across no man's land
The men tumble to the ground
And clog the Earth of no man's land.

The holes are big, the sloppy ground
Is all that is left of no man's land
Bodies here and the bodies there
Shows the destruction of no man's land.

Rory Purvis (13)
The Leys School, Cambridge

Court Martial

The rain fell like our men, hard and fast
Guns spluttered, always the relentless blast.
Down came the waterfalls of slime
Churning up the mud and grime.
Leaving pools of hate and fear
We could tell our end was drawing near.

On the face of my servant was a loving tear
'This is it,' he said, 'The end of my career.'
He will be court marshalled for leaving the others
But our hearts will remain with the mothers
Because they will forever mourn
For another thousand sons will be dead by dawn.

Jack Willmott (14)
The Leys School, Cambridge

On My Way To School

I walk out the door
A breeze of fresh air hit me in the face
Kids walking to school
I take a deep breath
Start walking to school
I see my bus
I run as fast as lightning
Finally
I made it
A bunch of school dudes on the bus
Walk upstairs
Top deck
I'm out of breath
Still can't believe I managed to catch the bus
Wow!
I'm at school
Schools gates close
I run before the
Gates close.
School has started
So I'm through with this
Poem.

Sediqah-Jaye Thompson-Miller (14)
The New Rush Hall School, Hainault

The Seasons

Everything's covered in a blanket of white
Tall bushy conifers stand in emerald might.
Soft flakes of cotton are drifting down
The pudding's in the oven, turning glistening brown.
The sky's grey and cloudy, people long for the sun
And the only thing that keeps them sane is snowy wintertime fun.

Emerald shavings cover all of the ground
The sweet sound of birdsong can be heard all around.
Small golden goblets turn their heads to the sun
All around are people enjoying warm happy fun.
No matter how hard you try, you can't have any strife
For spring is the time when earth's bursting with life.

Emerald hills roll for as far as the eye
Goblets cover the emerald reaching up high.
The wind's blowing gently, it sounds like a sigh,
No one can block the sunlight, no matter how hard they try.
The sun is on fire, the air's crackling with heat,
This is summer, the time when fire and Earth meet.

There are leaves on the ground, amber, crimson and gold,
It's getting colder - summer's warmth has decreased and grown old.
Chilled wind blows through the trees as they rustle and groan,
They shed their leaves in messy piles, making gardeners moan.
Earth's cycle goes on as the animals sleep,
This is autumn when Earth's treasure is harvested for keep.

Molly Coker (12)
The Philip Morant School & College, Colchester

If I Had A Time Machine . . .

If I had a time machine it would be pink.
It would be shaped like a telephone box
But when you walked in . . . the inside would be like a dream.
There would be a swimming pool in the library
And a city in the lounge, a shopping mall and restraint in the backyard.
If I had a time machine I could go to the moon and dodge things just like a spoon
It would fulfil all your hopes and all your dreams
And make bad things not what they seem.
If I had a time machine I'd visit Mars and eat lots of chocolate bars.
I'd go to the future and see what lies ahead and go back to the past and make all things right
So humans could live a happy life.
So if you like my little ride come on and jump inside and have the time of your life.

Larhys Skidmore (12)
Woodlands School, Basildon

If I Had A Time Machine . . .

If I had a time machine it would be square
And it would be blue and would be in my garden.
It would take me to different times and date and places.

If I had a time machine it would have buttons inside
And numbers so I could make a time and date
And the place that I was going to.

If I had a time machine I would visit the future in twenty years time
So I can see what I would look like and what my family looks like.

If I had a time machine I would go back to Australia in 2008
So I could see my relatives over there
And also to have another holiday over there because it is hot.

Alex Ronnie Alan Nicholson (12)
Woodlands School, Basildon

If I Had A Time Machine . . .

If I had a time machine I would change the world for the best and make a better place for all.
Then I would go to the Second World War and find out interesting facts.
Then I would go to the future to see what happens in my life and hope it turns out for the best.
After that I would go to the past and see Henry VIII and see if he was really fat or not!

Richard Langton (12)
Woodlands School, Basildon

If I Had A Time Machine . . .

If I had a time machine
The colour would be pink with two white stripes on the bonnet, white roof and shiny mirrors.
When you beep the horn the machine would take you into the future
And save people in trouble or from getting into trouble.
I would go anywhere, anytime.
I would make sure I complete my mission with everyone safe.

Cacey-Jayne Cox (12)
Woodlands School, Basildon

If I Had A Time Machine . . .

If I had a time machine it would look like a Mini Cooper with white stripes.
It would work when you pressed a date you wanted to go to.
If I could choose where I wanted to go it would be the future because I would want to see what happens
Also I would go to the past because I would like to remember my good times.

Keith King (11)
Woodlands School, Basildon

If I Had A Time Machine . . .

If I had a time machine it would be very big with big flashing lights on it.
It would spin around and around and take me anywhere I want.
If I had a time machine I would visit my children
Because I would like to see if they are good or bad
Then go home to have a nice cuppa.

Ashton Thomas Silk (11)
Woodlands School, Basildon

Young Writers Information

We hope you have enjoyed reading this book - and that you will continue to enjoy it in the coming years.

If you like reading and writing poetry drop us a line, or give us a call, and we'll send you a free information pack.

Alternatively if you would like to order further copies of this book or any of our other titles, then please give us a call or log onto our website at www.youngwriters.co.uk.

Young Writers Information
Remus House
Coltsfoot Drive
Peterborough
PE2 9JX
(01733) 890066